T4-AKG-642

HQ   Davey, Thomas,
792   1954-
.G3
D38   A generation
1987   divided

$29.95   Cop. 1

DATE			
AUG	1988		

WOODSON REGIONAL
LIBRARY CENTER
9525 SOUTH HALSTED STREET
CHICAGO, ILLINOIS 60628

© THE BAKER & TAYLOR CO.

R07127 75668

A
Generation
Divided

German Children and the Berlin Wall

Thomas Davey

Duke University Press
Durham 1987

ref
HQ
792
.G3
D38
1987
cop. 1

© 1987 Duke University Press
All rights reserved
Printed in the United States of America
on acid-free paper ∞

Library of Congress Cataloging-in-Publication Data
Davey, Thomas A., 1954–
 A generation divided.
 Bibliography: p.
 Includes index.
 1. Children—Berlin (Germany)—Social conditions.
 2. Children—Berlin (Germany)—Attitudes.
 3. Children—Berlin (Germany)—Psychology.
 I. Title.
HQ792.G3D38 1987   305.2'3'0943155 87-13497
ISBN 0-8223-0729-4

To my grandmother Estelle

To the children of East and West Berlin

Contents

Foreword

During one of her American visits Anna Freud spoke pointedly and eloquently about the possibilities for future research by those who are trained to work with children. She emphasized in her talk the need for ongoing clinical studies—efforts to learn what goes wrong in the psychological lives of particular children and what might be done to help those boys and girls get on better emotionally. But she took pains to challenge some of us listening to her with a further suggestion: "We need to learn more about the way children respond to the world outside the home—the pressures upon them, and their response to those pressures. The direct observation of children in our clinics ought be extended to schools and playgrounds, to homes—naturalistic direct observation as a companion to clinical direct observation. There is always time (and inclination!) for theoretical speculation and elaboration; but we must keep asking, first, for careful description of what has been seen and heard, for careful attention to the details of a child's ongoing life in one or another social situation. There will be plenty of time, later, to assess the relative significance for each boy or girl of the 'internal' as against the 'external'— the pressure of the 'instincts' as against the pressure of the 'society.' We need to explore before we conclude!"

Were she alive today Miss Freud would surely be captivated by this particular exploration—an extraordinarily vigorous and resourceful effort by a young and talented child psychologist to learn how a serious and continuing political confrontation, concretely symbolized in the well-known form of the wall that divides the city of Berlin, affects the everyday emotional life of the children who live near a monument of sorts to our human capacity to set ourselves ever so militantly apart from one another. Indeed, the political tensions in Berlin resonate all too obviously with those childhood struggles we have learned in this century to take so seriously—the growth in our sons and daughters of strong attachments, but also persistent antagonisms, suspicions, fears. It is as if Berlin's fate has been to remind us, yet again, what our psychological makeup yearns to express—strong loyalties, but also relentless apprehensions and misgivings.

Nor do our children fail to take note of what the so-called adult world chooses (or is driven) to do, as this book shows so clearly, so carefully. The Berlin Wall for countless boys and girls has become a persisting and inviting presence—a summons of sorts: here is what the grown-up world has done; now let me take heed, take stock, and fit what I have noticed into my own appraisal of the world. Again and again the German children whom Dr. Davey came to know so well—through months and months of Anna Freud's "naturalistic direct observation"—have made clear to him, and through this book to all of us, how pointedly and searchingly young people can respond to what we adults call "social problems" or "politics" or "ideological struggles." Hence the value of this research, not only for psychiatrists and psychologists but for the social sciences and, yes, for all who are interested in the way political tensions work their way into the lives of ordinary human beings.

This book offers stories, really, illustrated stories: boys and girls telling of their thoughts, their hopes and dreams, their worries and fears, and not least, their moments of amusement, of sadness, of wry resignation to the dreary, powerful implacability of the so-called adult world. At times, actually, this book offers poetry—brief, condensed, highly charged and suggestive lyrical outbursts: particular boys or girls turning a dramatic and forceful aspect of the world's "reality" into a metaphor of sorts. The Berlin Wall becomes for those children what New England fences and stone walls become for Robert Frost, a philosophical and psychological artifact of considerable daily authority. I fear that those of us who work with children have tended to overlook this capacity—this strong interest, really—of theirs: to attend the physical characteristics of the city-scape, the countryside, and to analyze the symbolic aspects of those characteristics. Just as children have often pointed out to me that one kind of person dresses this way, lives in that kind of dwelling, prefers such-and-such cars—and for reasons I have then heard spelled out—the Berliners whom we meet in this book have figured out what the world-famous wall, now a quarter of a century old, has to tell us about Washington and Moscow, about capitalism and communism, about all sorts of social and economic and political matters, about the workings of history itself.

Nor ought we overlook the willingness of these children to stop and reflect upon the rights and wrongs of the world—an ethical analysis that keeps asserting itself, implicitly or explicitly. Those who built the Berlin Wall, and those who are horrified and disgusted by it, or try to flee past it, have in their minds what is good or bad, desirable or thoroughly unattractive with respect to the world. Children are not by any means beyond a comprehension of such a morality, at once political and personal, in the sense that nationalist sentiments or ideological agendas have a way of working themselves into the assumptions of a family, parents and children alike. In a sense, then, this study is a documentary effort on the part of a child psychologist to learn about the complex relationship between politics and moral perception in childhood—carried out in a concrete set of circumstances especially intriguing and challenging.

Needless to say, only a certain kind of researcher or fieldworker could have accomplished the ambitious project this book describes. I do not exaggerate when I mention the courage required—the tact and patience and daring involved in going back and forth, back and forth, through the very wall, the quiet dangerous wall, which these children have tried in their various ways to comprehend. East Berlin is no "open city," nor are its citizens always free to speak and act as they wish. This study offers eloquent testimony, therefore, of what a dedicated psychological observer can achieve—a long and hard glimpse at what otherwise gets hidden by force. The result of Tom Davey's hard work, sensitive observations, and strong, clear writing is this book, of course, but something else, too—an instance of what psychological research or documentary studies can become at their best: a kind of powerful, compelling moral witness.

Robert Coles, M.D.

Acknowledgments

This has been a collaborative effort from the very start. Without the help from friends and colleagues in this country and in East and West Berlin, this work could not have been completed. To begin, I want to thank Robert Coles for his friendship and support over the years. By his example he has been a constant inspiration and source of strong encouragement. I also thank Dean Whitla for his generosity and perceptive critical eye.

I want to acknowledge my friends in this country whose patience, encouragement, and love constantly helped me along with this project. I mention them together and trust that each of them knows the very special way in which he or she has been there for me: Barbara Kivowitz, Becky Novotny, Frank McCauley, Jon Wight, Matthew Gilbert, Rick Weissbourd, Sara McLeod, Tom Fox, and Margaret Plank.

I must thank many people in both East and West Berlin—especially the children who taught me so much and gave so freely of themselves in circumstances not always so amenable to such generosity of spirit. Unfortunately, I cannot mention by name my friends in East Berlin, and I only hope that one day that will be possible. In West Berlin, I was constantly helped, both professionally and personally, by the following individuals: Roswitha Zirk; Roni and Lilo Galle and their two children, Claudine and Fabi; Herr Seidl, Frau Schultz, and Frau Rehyse, of the Möwensee Grundschule. I also mention three friends: Anya Kolcz, Frank Kretschmer, and Maria Valiante.

This work would not have gotten off the ground, however, without the generous financial support of the German Academic Exchange Service during my year in Berlin and the continuing support of the Lyndhurst Foundation. I am extremely indebted to both of these institutions.

I would also like to thank Joanne Ferguson of Duke University Press for her sound critical advice.

Finally, I wish to thank my mother and father, and brothers and sisters, for their abiding love and support.

1 | Introduction

Long before "political socialization" became designated a field of study and part of the domain of psychologists and social scientists, philosophers and political thinkers were asking how it is that children come to feel themselves members of a particular political system. Plato's *Republic* asserts that the state must take an active interest in the upbringing of children, whom Plato perceives first and foremost as future citizens. Rousseau addressed the relationship between family life, schooling, and the larger society in *Emile,* as well as in his posthumously published *The Government of Poland* ("When a Pole reaches the age of twenty, he must be a Pole, not some other kind of man.").[1] Another Frenchman, Napoléon, remarked in 1808 that "as long as children are not taught whether they ought to be Republican or Monarchist, Catholic or irreligious, the State will not form a Nation."[2] How does this process of becoming a member of a particular nation—with its unique history, preoccupations, ideals—get under way? And how best to examine childhood in such a light?

I asked these and related questions in the striking world of East and West Berlin, where two deeply opposed political systems (sprung from a unified German nation more than forty years ago) confront one another so visibly and unrelentingly. There I spoke with children living on either side of the Berlin Wall, in the hopes of better understanding the sense they make of the efforts of their respective nations—The German Democratic Republic and the Federal Republic of Germany—to secure the allegiance of their children. These are young people who share a linguistic, cultural, and historical heritage, as well as family ties that transcend political borders. Yet they are coming of age in two radically different political and economic systems. How do they come to terms, emotionally and cognitively, with this unique, frequently painful and frustrating reality? What are the lessons intended for them? And what are the lessons they in fact learn? How do these children persist as *Germans* while at the same time becoming something else—*socialist* or *capitalist* Germans?

This is the first generation of Germans to grow up with the Berlin Wall. They know nothing, through experience, of a physically undivided Berlin. They are left to grapple with the questions such a stark reality elicits from them. In so doing, they make observations that illuminate their political, moral, and psychological concerns. What or who does this barrier keep out, or protect us from? What is included within its reach? Who are we, and what do we believe in—as opposed to those people "over there"? In their efforts to address these questions, children look carefully at their surroundings, listen to what they are taught (formally and informally), and often find themselves somewhere between the demands of rhetoric and the persuasiveness of experience.

Certainly I chose an environment that by no means can be considered "normal" or representative of cities elsewhere in the Federal Republic of Germany (the FRG, or West Germany) or the German Democratic Republic (GDR, or East Germany). These are indeed special political circumstances in which these children find themselves. It appeared likely to me that here certain aspects of the child's developing sense of ideological and national allegiances might stand out in sharp relief. Nowhere else in either nation is a child confronted so early with such a striking manifestation of East-West political divisiveness. Yet, as Freud knew, a careful consideration of pathology can be useful in illuminating the vicissitudes of normalcy. Likewise, I suspect that a clearer understanding of childhood in extreme conditions might also offer us a greater appreciation of the political and moral life of children elsewhere.

I decided to spend my time with latency-age children—ten to twelve years old, by and large. Though certainly not a period of visible Sturm und Drang as can be the later, adolescent years, this is nonetheless a very crucial period in the child's life when he is beginning to make increasingly complex connections with the larger social world.[3] Anna Freud refers to latency as "the post-oedipal lessening of drive urgency and the transfer of libido from the parental figures to contemporaries, community groups, teachers, leaders, impersonal ideals, and aim-inhibited, sublimated interests."[4] In his extensive work with children in this country and abroad,

Robert Coles has pointed again and again to the fact that young children are not only able but quite willing to maintain an active involvement with the world of politics and ideology.[5]

I felt it was important to continue looking at this period of the child's life in "the field" in order to better understand the process whereby children come to feel increasingly related to their social and political milieu. How do children make use of the particular elements of political life in a setting as ideologically charged as that of Berlin, East and West? How do they use or discard various pieces of information in their efforts to establish an allegiance to their group? In such a setting do children readily establish national or ideological allegiances, or do they develop a more ambivalent sense of national or ideological affiliation?

There is a growing body of research devoted to various aspects of the child's "political socialization" that is widely divergent in focus and theoretical conceptualization. Researchers have looked at the relationship between family life and the child's acquisition of political values; they have examined the impact of formal education and the media on these same values. At the same time, several researchers have tended to limit their discussion to elements of the child's political life that can be "measured" in some fashion.[6] They speak of the child's "sense of political efficacy," or of the child's "attitudes toward political authority," or "party identification." Not surprisingly, attempts to isolate specific sources of political and ideological influence have revealed the fairly conservative influence exerted by any one source, be it family, school, or the media. Common sense, along with close observation of children, points to the need for careful scrutiny of a range of such "influences"—family, education, social class, media, historical and political circumstances—as they bear down on children. This is a herculean task, yet one that approaches the complex reality of the political life of children.

I discovered in the field how difficult it is to establish a firm correspondence between the "message" children receive from various "sources" and the political views of those children. In addition, it became clear that an "agent of political socialization" that may be especially influential in East Berlin may play a relatively negligible role in West Berlin, and vice versa. For example, the fact that western television programs can be picked up in East Berlin homes is of enormous significance for the development of political beliefs held by East Berlin youngsters. In addition, the Lutheran church in East Germany plays a very important role in encouraging young people to experience and express (within the safety of a church group) their decidedly mixed feelings toward the East German state.

Although this is primarily a study of the ways children make sense of their political world, as opposed to a study intent on isolating and examining specific "agents" of political socialization, I did hear again and again from these children about the importance to them of this or that "outside influence." In both cities children referred directly or indirectly to the family, the school, and the face of a city as it reflects history and politics: monuments, scars from the last war, and most importantly, the Berlin Wall. In East Berlin, children also spoke frequently of the significance of television and the Lutheran church. I would like to examine briefly a few of these here, before turning to the children themselves.

Family life undoubtedly exerts its influence on the child's larger political views, along with his sense of being a member of a particular national community. This is especially evident in East Berlin, where the family unit often manages to serve as a bulwark against state intrusiveness. Various studies of the relationship between the child's experience within the family and his feelings toward political authority figures serve as an illuminating backdrop for my observations in the capital city of East Germany. Some of these studies suggest that young children express great faith in important political figures on account of their great identification with parental authority, along with an inability to disengage one kind of authority from another. Positive feelings for the political authority figure appear to be rooted in positive familial experiences.[7] Yet not all research has confirmed these findings, and some studies indicate that under certain circumstances (political, socioeconomic, historical) children may express quite different feelings toward political authority figures.[8] These studies dismiss the simplistic correlation between positive family experience and positive regard for political authority as most likely the product of exclusive reliance on middle-class, urban children.[9] Also, many of the studies mentioned are concerned with American children.

In my work in East Berlin, I found that the situation can be very different when the children studied live in political systems where the leadership is not considered particularly benign and is not perceived as representative of the people. A child's views of political authority *may* reflect positive experience with parental authority, assuming that the political authority does deliver on its promises and can be fairly readily identified with parental authority. The relationship between family and regime becomes more complicated when, as is often the case in East Berlin, the gap between family values and regime values is fairly wide.

Because of the political system that obtains in East Germany, one that is extremely resistant to scrutiny by outsiders, very few studies of children have been conducted in that nation. Those that have been carried out generally serve to illuminate the state's efforts at winning the allegiance of children, but it has proven difficult to ascertain the effectiveness of those efforts.[10] Certainly there are many obstacles to just such an understanding, not the least of them being the well-documented "socialist schizophrenia,"[11] whereby the individual may hold "politically incorrect" personal opinions side by side with "correct" political philosophy. It takes time and a good deal of mutual trust for an investigator to begin to distinguish the two lines of thought—two lines of *being*, really. As this trust developed between me and the children and families I came to know, I began to see how many parents encourage in their children an outward acceptance of the regime coupled with a more guarded personal assessment. The issue for them is less one of ideological conviction and much more one of survival—personal and professional. Rather than providing a strong foundation of support for government values, the family unit often serves as a counterpoint of deep personal resistance. What is extraordinary to observe are the ways children learn, at a very early age, to juggle the "personal" and the "political" (which are not always diametrically opposed). And these are lessons gleaned in good part from the family.

Other lessons are, of course, acquired in the schools, although in many instances the lessons learned are not the lessons intended. The educational systems in East and West Berlin have set very different agendas for themselves, although the assumption underlying those agendas is shared: that the school is an extremely important setting in which to inculcate in children nationally desirable beliefs. A number of researchers have devoted attention to the significance of formal education in the child's acquisition of political values.[12] In his valuable, immensely readable portrait of the modernization of rural France, Eugene Weber states that "the school . . . compulsory and free, has been credited with the ultimate acculturation process that made the French people French."[13] And Urie Bronfenbrenner notes the tremendous value that the Soviet authorities invest in education; he suggests that the schools, through behavioral techniques as well as textbooks, do an impressive job of inculcating certain desired qualities— ideological, social, personal—in children.[14]

My work in Berlin suggests that children are sifting and weighing various pieces of information that they pick up in the school—each of them making somewhat different sense of it all, according to his or her particular circumstances. Certainly the formal curriculum varies considerably between East and West Berlin, reflecting the vastly different values of the two nations. Although such differences will be most visibly expressed in history, government, and economics classes, they appear even in apparently unrelated courses such as math and science, music and art. A typical problem in an East German fourth-year math textbook asks the student to calculate the difference in military strength between opposing socialist and capitalist armies. Extracurricular activities are also avenues of political and ideological instruction. On top of that, children can be very responsive to the informal curriculum in school: not simply *what* the teacher says, but how he or she says it. For example, although there is no clear and unified approach in West Germany to teaching about the Second World War and the Holocaust (so that, in fact, very little gets taught), many teachers nonetheless try to convey to children their lack of responsibility for what happened forty years ago. Yet a number of teachers have difficulty themselves with the subject, and their own hesitations and feelings of guilt and responsibility are frequently apparent to their young students, who are then left to struggle with these conflicting messages.

And in East Berlin, children are constantly witnesses to the politics of power within the classroom. They learn early about the ways fellow students are variously punished or rewarded for the manner in which they express their views (personal and political) in school. They are taught about the concern their government, along with local authorities, has for ordinary people ("comrades") like themselves; yet they see just how serious the consequences can be for even minor infractions of the ideological rules. Over the years, then, these children are learning lessons that do not always coincide with their formal lessons—lessons that teach them about the realities of being East as opposed to West Germans.

One must keep in mind that schools are part of a larger culture, and the messages children acquire in school are often contradicted by messages coming from other quarters. In his study of French village life Laurence Wylie sheds light on this very issue: "In preaching civic virtue to the school children, the authors of the civics book recognize that their precepts describe an ideal rather than an actual state of things. . . . Yet the children constantly hear adults referring to government as a source of evil and to the men who run it as instruments of evil. There is nothing personal in this belief. It does not concern one particular government. . . . It concerns government everywhere, and at all times."[15] This is an important reminder of the lopsided view one gets when trying to isolate one or another element of the child's life from its larger context, that is, the complex life of the child himself.

One of those other "elements" to consider is the role of the media. Although it is not clear how pivotal television is for West Berlin children, it was dramatically apparent just how influential that medium is for the children and young people of East Berlin. There, with easy access to televised programming from West Berlin, children are forcefully confronted with political views and social perspectives diametrically opposed to those espoused in their schools and in the national media. Many children with whom I spoke pointed to television as their primary source of information not only about the West, but about their own nation as well. It provides them with perspectives unavailable to them elsewhere and puts them in a position to weigh several points of view outside the reach of the official view. As these children reveal in their comments, such a position is by no means a comfortable one.

I do not claim to have conducted a formal study of television viewing in East and West Berlin (nor of education, or the family). Yet I would concur with two studies that have managed to take the discussion of the relationship between television viewing and the child's political views beyond the narrow confines within which so much of the related research is conducted.[16] Wallace Lambert and Otto Klineberg, in their provocative study of the views of children toward other nations, found that television was an oft-cited source of information used by children in developing their opinions about foreign people. And R.W. Connell, who has done remarkable work with Australian children, suggests that television viewing disrupts what he sees to be a developmental progression of political awareness— starting with an awareness of local community, then of region, and finally of native country and other nations—and instead introduces children to the full range of global politics at once. They come to know about—and react to emotionally—events that are both far removed from their lives and out of the control of those around them. This is no doubt as true for children in West Berlin as for those in the neighboring city of East Berlin. Yet the crucial difference has to do with whether and how television programming supports or undermines a nation's stated values. In East Berlin, where there is little unequivocal support for the government, western television serves to further erode the generally ambivalent support of many young people.

Finally, at least as far as this brief discussion is concerned, there is the Lutheran church in East Berlin. It is impossible to speak of the "political socialization" of young people in East Germany without making mention of the church. It is an institution which plays a role that is possible only in a politically repressive society like East Germany. In West Berlin, as in a good number of western democracies, freedom of faith, along with the lack of any clear-cut adversarial position for the church to take, may minimize the potency—politically and in the minds of children—of any particular religious group. Unlike the Catholic church in Poland, the Lutheran church is not so much seen as the institutional embodiment of the German state (the "true" German state, the German soul); rather, it is widely viewed as the institution that nurtures the human spirit in the face of a repressive, bureaucratic regime, as well as the institution that, against great odds, demands that the government account for itself. During my stay in the city (1981–82), the church's clear support of the struggling peace movement within East Germany gave it even more visibility, and it became increasingly an institution sought after by young people looking to find their way within the confines of a controlled political society.

Again, this is not a quantitative study of various "agents of political socialization." I am far more interested in the ways certain children make sense of their political and national predicament—really, their existential predicament. Connell speaks of the "child's construction of politics"—a very apt phrase that points up the fact that children do not simply absorb and regurgitate information about their political world and their relationship with it. Rather, they are engaged in an extended, frequently confusing process of sorting out that information in order to develop their own unique understanding—to establish their place in their world.[17] The "direct observation" relied on by Anna Freud[18] allowed me to hear from children ideas and sentiments otherwise not offered to adults, especially those who are relative strangers. The reality of the Wall, probably the most significant political and existential reality to be faced by the children of Berlin, might suggest to the outside observer that the issues with which these young people contend are indeed black or white. Yet the fact is that ambivalence reigns in both these cities—especially among their children. Issues here are not at all clear-cut, nor are they as easily formulated as the unavoidable fact of the Wall (and official rhetoric on both sides) would suggest.

The children with whom I spoke came from a variety of backgrounds, and they insistently reminded me that their responses to a fairly striking political situation were their own, not always amenable to the confines of theory, nor to the expectations of the observer. Their words are strong evidence of the complexity not only of the political *situation* in which they find themselves—the various influences brought to bear on their young lives—but also of their political and moral *life*—how they weave into whole cloth the diverse strands of experience. One twelve-year-old East Berlin boy rather angrily reprimanded me when, early on in our relationship, it became apparent that I presumed his dissatisfaction with life in the East. "I'm tired of everyone in the West thinking we're unhappy here! Everyone over there wants to believe we hate it here—but I think they just want to feel better about themselves. Sometimes you see these people come over from West Berlin, and they have their BMW, or their nice clothes, and they look at us like they feel sorry for us! And I think, maybe they should feel sorry for themselves sometimes! I'm not saying I love it here all the time. Sometimes I do want to leave, look around. But I *can't*. And even if I could, this is my home; and I would return here if I left. And I don't want people insulting my home."

His is hardly an isolated sentiment among the young East Berliners I knew: an abiding resentment toward others who pass quick judgments without taking the time to understand. It is a defensiveness with several roots: the need to come to terms with and appreciate some aspects of a life that cannot be escaped; the knowledge that there are praiseworthy elements to East German life (material and moral); the feeling that this is home, "the place of my parents and friends," and hence deserving of some allegiance; and finally, and importantly, a sense that each nation has its difficulties, and that in no place is paradise to be found.

Similarly, in West Berlin I was rebuked, somewhat indirectly, by an eleven-year-old girl living in the working class district of Wedding. "Sometimes I go down to Ku'damm [Kurfürstendamm] with my mother, and I see all those tourists and all those expensive shops and nightclubs and I get mad, because I think they think all of us in Berlin are like those rich people there. Well we're not, and I don't want to be either. I'm not saying we're poor, just that we're not rich like some of them, either. Sometimes I think there are really two Berlins. No, I don't mean East and West Berlin. I mean two *West* Berlins: the rich Berlin that everyone wants to see, and then us." This girl points out that her city has other boundaries (established, in this instance, along the fault line of class) just as significant for her as that better-publicized one between East and West Berlin.

The reader will notice that these Berlin youngsters speak of their

political and national (that is, personal) predicament with a distinct eloquence and an apparent sophistication that clearly sets them apart from,
say, their American peers. Certain theorists posit a stagelike progression in
the development of political and ideological understanding which might
not always allow young children the possibility of a complex engagement
with these realities.[19] Yet in my work in nations where serious political and
moral struggles are part of the child's daily fare—South Africa, Northern
Ireland, Poland, and now East and West Berlin[20]—I have noticed that children are forced to come to terms with that reality earlier than their
contemporaries in environments less politically volatile.[21] They learn early
what and *who* works for or against them. Certainly it is these kinds of
observations, in East and West Berlin, that are of enormous importance to
children and their families.

What these young people have to say is frequently moving. Many of
them find themselves in a complex situation, with very mixed allegiances
toward their respective nations. By and large I heard them express not only
an understandable ambivalence, but a sense of pain and betrayal over the
circumstances that arouse such mixed feelings. These are children who
avidly seek after something worthy of their loyalty; it does matter to them
that they be able to rely on the authorities in charge and to feel some pride
in belonging to a particular national community. In West Berlin, however,
children speak of their pain over an ugly national past. They find it impossible to dissociate themselves from the Nazi period in their nation's life,
despite the obvious fact that they came into this world much later. And in
East Berlin, where that same past is in some respects less of a burden
(pawned off, as it were, onto West Germany), children are all too aware of
the many restrictions they face—restrictions embodied all too clearly in
the fact of the Berlin Wall. Many of these youngsters look to the West in a
persistent effort at maintaining a sense of pride in being *German,* at least
(as opposed to being simply a GDR citizen, which is how they are encouraged to see themselves). In both cities of Berlin, the Wall is an unavoidable
reminder of some very painful historical and political *and* familial facts,
and it cuts away at the pride these young people might feel in their respective nations and hence at their own sense of self-worth.

Contemporary theorists John Mack and Vamik Volkan suggest that the
individual forges a positive link between the self and the larger group (or
nation) by investing that group with the ego ideal—that aspect of the individual ego wherein all of one's good and loving feelings and aspirations are
maintained, the better part of oneself.[22] Mack goes on to suggest that a

person's most profound values and ideals may be associated with what his nation represents, and that "self regard may rise and fall with the fate of one's nation."[23] Volkan points out that this positive identification with one's own nation may require another group "out there" on which to externalize "bad" self and object representations. "We are good because we are not like 'them.' " Certainly the Wall, because of its function as well as its sheer visibility, can encourage just such externalization on the part of children in the cities to either side of it. As one young man told me, "We need our enemies."

Yet this neat rendering of "us" and "them" proves somewhat less helpful in the long run. Because of the complex relationship between their two nations, one that includes family ties across clearly demarcated ideological boundaries, these children find such a rigidly dichotomous view impossible to maintain. Antipathy toward the other side (exaggerated in the East Berlin schools and underplayed in West Berlin, where hopes for a reunification are still voiced and a recognition of common German roots is emphasized) is often tempered by an awareness of a shared German heritage. Most children speak of one German nation, two German states; and they struggle to negotiate their way between the distance that open ideological conflict demands and the feelings of relatedness that an appreciation of common national roots encourages. In other words, aside from the day-to-day lessons they learn within the home, these young people's views are also shaped by the fact of family existing, *enduring* across a hostile, arbitrary border. There is nothing abstract about this, inasmuch as many children on either side of the Wall can name at least one relative living "over there": a grandparent, an aunt, an uncle. One young West Berlin boy, when asked about the cause for the division of Germany and the subsequent building of the Wall, said: "I know that Berlin and Germany used to be one nation, but I'm really not sure why there are two Germanys now. I think that there were families fighting with each other, and they couldn't get along, so they built the Wall." This boy is expressing, albeit somewhat more concretely, what many of his peers feel: that the division of a nation was and remains a family matter—not at all an abstract political matter. How will the next generation of children feel when those personal ties have all but disappeared?

The regard these children hold for their own as well as the "other" Berlin hinges, too, on the manner in which security and freedom are balanced. These youngsters are constantly assessing their personal lives, along with their larger national life, in terms of the kind of control brought to bear on the individual. It became clear in our conversations that most children require a balance of control (safety) and freedom, in varying proportions. For many West Berlin children, "drüben," or "over there," has too much control, yet also has the advantage of being more peaceful—a more "rural," less stressful environment. In contrast, they frequently perceive their own city as offering freedom but occasionally lacking sufficient controls—a city that can often erupt into frightening displays of aggression: demonstrations were almost a daily occurrence during my stay in West Berlin.

East Berlin children, on the other hand, often describe their nation as repressive in regard to expression of personal freedoms such as freedom of speech and freedom to travel. Yet they are also offered safety from the apparent chaos of the West (witnessed on television and exaggerated in official rhetoric). Many of these young people feel that with too much freedom come dangerous manifestations of aggression, resulting in an abiding feeling of insecurity.

In fact, the issue of safety is of considerable importance. Along with its other meanings, the Wall serves as the border between two hostile armies, each of them well equipped and capable of inflicting great harm on the other. With this clearly in mind, children express feelings of obligation toward and some identification with the political entity that serves to protect them. West Berlin children often speak more highly of the United States than of West Germany; after all, they say, it is the United States that "will protect us from our enemies"—particularly the Soviet Union. Of course, this praise was offered up with ambivalence, since concern over the stationing of American missiles on West German soil was very much on people's minds (and highlighted their fears of vulnerability, dread of war, and feelings of impotence vis-à-vis America) during the period of my stay.

When East Berlin children praise their nation, it is for the security offered—both in terms of military protection as well as certain material guarantees: jobs, housing, medicine. Although they are educated to regard the Soviet Union with warmth and camaraderie, children learn early to temper that regard, if not to abandon it altogether. They certainly experience their own struggles—as individuals and as a nation—with the fact of an occupying power.

Finally, I feel it is important to make quite clear that these children also present a moral response to the reality defined by the Berlin Wall. Although they will frequently "use" their knowledge of life "on the other side" in order to enhance their appreciation of their own city and nation, they will also use that knowledge as a tool for self-scrutiny and self-criticism. Children may initially respond to the material discrepancies between nations, but they are also willing to demonstrate a sense of justice and fair play. They struggle with the differing intentions of the two political systems and the gap between intention and practice (for example, what provisions are made for the poor; who earns how much and why). Rather than "projecting" all badness onto the other side, as Volkan saw happening in Cyprus (where the struggle is between two distinct national groups, where "ambiguities of good and evil are difficult to see"),[24] many of these German children are quite able to recognize and grapple with the ambiguity of their predicament, as well as the ambivalence of their own feelings.

This is an extended essay on the manner in which history and politics become elements of personal psychology. It is an effort to document a complicated political reality as it is experienced by young children presumably growing up to become members of one or another political system. These are children who, unlike their parents or grandparents, have grown up with the Wall. They have never known life without it. It is not only a rather overwhelming reality, but is a powerful symbol too. As such, it captures the imagination of the children living on either side of it and inspires them to look carefully at their surroundings, and to ask some very hard questions—of themselves and their parents, and of their nations.

2 | Berlin

Berlin emerged in the twelfth century as a "double town," divided by geography rather than ideology. To the east of the River Spree lay Berlin, a community of merchants, while to the west lay Cölln, a town of fishermen. From those origins grew a town of great political, economic, and cultural significance—all of which can be attributed in good part to the city's location. Berlin lies in the center of Europe, and hence felt the influence of the steady streams of merchants and other travelers making their way from the various corners of Europe. By the 1930s the city was the largest train juncture on the continent, while river traffic from France to points east, as well as from Scandinavia to western and southern Europe regularly crossed on the Spree, running through the heart of Berlin. By that time it had grown to be the most densely populated city of Germany, as well as the largest industrial center between Paris and Moscow. In geographic terms, the city was (and remains) enormous: owing to a move to absorb outlying suburbs into the city proper in the 1920s, the dimensions of Berlin grew to an impressive 88,000 hectares.

Berlin has always been regarded by the people of the various German states—both prior to and following unification—with marked ambivalence. Throughout much of its history Germany was only a patchwork of rancorous principalities that defied any effort to consolidate such diversity under the banner of one nation. In such a situation, provincialism reigned. And as a relatively cosmopolitan city, inviting the presence and influence of various outsiders, among them Jews and Huguenots, Berlin was suspect. Further complicating the city's image was its position as capital of Prussia—a state that, by virtue of its power and influence, was resented (as well as grudgingly respected) by a good portion of the German population. Prussia managed to combine an extreme militarism, which was supported by an ethic of obedience to authority (crucial for successful unification, and often pointed to as the foundation for the later abuses of Nazism), with a deep albeit sporadic interest in and support of the arts and intellectual life. As its capital city, Berlin was the seat of authority and power and also attracted a wide range of artists and intellectuals; at one point it was referred to as the Athens on the Spree (Spreeathen).[1] At the close of the First World War, the city became the center for the German experiment with democracy—the short-lived Weimar Republic. Immediately thereafter, it took on its most notorious identity—as the capital of the Third Reich. As such, the word *Berlin* became synonymous with words such as *fascism* and *oppression,* and associated with names like Hitler, Speer, Hess—the henchmen of Nazi Germany.

Subsequent to the destruction of the German nation in 1945 by the Allied powers, the city lay in rubble. Modest estimates put the ruin of pre-war industrial Berlin at 75 to 85 percent.[2] Initially parceled into four sectors, each administered by the conquering powers—the United States, France, Great Britain, and the Soviet Union—the city was soon pulled apart by ideological forces. West Berlin fell under Allied influence, while East Berlin and the rest of the Soviet zone of occupation became a permanent part of the Soviet Bloc. Once the city from which the two great wars were waged, divided Berlin was now at the heart of the cold war.

Periodically the reality of this political rift has been greatly dramatized. In the summer of 1948 the Soviets initiated the Berlin Blockade, whereby all traffic arteries connecting West Berlin to the western-occupied zones of the nation were severed. The western allies responded with the "Luftbrücke," flying in food and other essentials on a nonstop schedule until the lifting of the blockade during the spring of the following year.

A decade later, West Berlin's "island" status was once again highlighted by the "Khrushchev Ultimatum," as the Soviet Union demanded the total abdication of the city by all non-German troops. The Allied troops didn't move, and the ultimatum was rescinded a month later. Finally, on August 13, 1961, it became impossible to pretend that the reunification of this city, let alone that of the divided German nation, would come soon or easily. On that day GDR soldiers began sealing off East Berlin from West Berlin—first with coils of barbed wire, later with concrete. This was the beginning of the Berlin Wall, which remains today—surrounding West Berlin and reinforced with increasingly sophisticated military technology.

The Wall

The Wall was built for a very specific reason: to stem the flow of esca-
pees ("Flüchtlinge") from the German Democratic Republic into the
West, via West Berlin. From the year 1949 to that August day in 1961,
more than 2.5 million people had fled the GDR for the West; and of those,
more than 1.5 million had entered West Berlin.[3] In spite of the already
well-established political (and economic and social) differences between
the two cities of Berlin prior to the construction of the Wall, the border
between them was still permeable. Residents from the East were able to
hold jobs in West Berlin and to visit friends and family there. The Wall
immediately divided the two cities physically, leaving many individuals
suddenly and irrevocably separated from their kin on the other side. Since
the Wall's construction, along with the tightening of the German-German
border, there has been a significant drop in successful escapes. In 1980,
only three thousand people managed to leave for the West, and the vast
majority of those did so through other countries, such as Yugoslavia.[4]
Along the Wall seventy-three people have been killed since 1961, and
today that border is virtually impregnable.[5]

Although the Wall was designed to prevent individuals from leaving the
East, it encircles West Berlin, accentuating the "island mentality" of the
residents of that city. Altogether it is approximately 170 kilometers in cir-
cumference, and most of that is a twelve-foot-high reinforced concrete
wall topped with a curved concrete "cap." At certain points the Wall is
replaced with a wire netting fence and barbed wire, although soon the concrete wall will be visible from virtually any point in West Berlin, barring
waterways. Behind this primary wall, which wends its way in a seemingly
arbitrary manner between East and West Berlin, lies the expanse of "no-
man's-land." Here the visitor, standing on one of the one hundred viewing
platforms erected in West Berlin for just this purpose, can see the assorted
border paraphernalia: watchtowers, guard dog runs, mine fields, GDR border patrols (on foot or in vehicles), antitank devices and, most recently,
automatic shooting devices that are tripped by the movements of the
potential escapee. To the far side of this space (almost one hundred meters
wide) is yet another wall. It is this less imposing structure that the citizen
of the GDR might come up against, though unless he lives in the vicinity of
the border, police are quick to interrupt his unauthorized presence.

Although most West Berliners would argue that they have accustomed
themselves all too well to the Wall, it exerts a definite influence on them

nonetheless: "Mauerkrankheit" (Wall sickness) is the frequent explanation given for a person's particular bouts of moodiness. Now and again one reads in the paper of some disconsolate individual ramming his car full speed into the Wall as a means to suicide. Occasionally the Wall can appear to be just another part of the city's architectural landscape, scrawled over with graffiti, or sporting a particularly colorful mural. It is when a street that once led into East Berlin dead-ends into the Wall, or is literally divided down the middle, as is Bernauerstrasse, that the Wall is dramatically *present*. Yet it is even more striking and out of place in the more sparsely populated districts of West Berlin, such as the village of Lübars to the north. There the Wall looms bright white in contrast to the rolling fields and pastures through which it cuts its way.

In East Berlin it is likely that most residents rarely encounter the border. Yet it is embarrassingly obvious when viewed from the revolving restaurant atop the television tower in the heart of Alexanderplatz. Herein lies one of numerous ironies: the people of East Berlin are best able to see the precise nature of their constraints (the Wall) from the pride of GDR officialdom (the television tower).

On the occasion of the twentieth anniversary of the building of the Wall, East Berlin and West Berlin demonstrated very different responses to that moment in history. In West Berlin the senate allowed for a period of quiet reflection, and there was a laying of wreaths at the numerous crosses alongside the Wall—crosses in memory of individuals who have died either trying to escape the East or trying to abet an escape. And along the fashionable Kurfürstendamm young people staged a silent protest march.

To the other side of the Wall the day was welcomed with a military parade in which ten thousand soldiers of the National People's Army participated, along with the members of other defense organizations. In the textbooks of East German children the Wall is described as a necessary defense measure. Here is an example of a fourth-grade history text:

> The Capitalists and the ruling powers in West Germany have tried from the beginning to prevent our Republic from becoming wealthy and strong. With every available means they've attempted to destroy our efforts at rebuilding our nation. Especially before August 13, 1961, they took advantage of the open border between the capital of the German Democratic Republic and West Berlin, in order to carry out their plans. They sent spies and government agents into our country, who were to spread lies about our Republic. They were also assigned to carry out

destructive activities, and to try to attract engineers, doctors, and skilled workers to West Germany. They allowed goods, desired over there—goods that were also very much needed by our people—to be bought from our stores and brought to West Berlin: cameras, binoculars, textiles, and foodstuffs.

In 1961 the warmongers in West Germany increasingly prepared themselves to conquer the GDR. They agitated against our nation and insulted it. With the help of its allies, West Germany initiated military maneuvers along the border of the GDR. They often spoke of violently usurping our GDR. In other words, they wanted to set back the achievements of the Worker and Farmer State, which had arisen out of very difficult reconstruction efforts. That, however, would have meant war. The plans of the warmongers had to be prevented.

On the night of August 12–13, 1961, the end of these plans of the ruling powers in the Federal Republic of Germany were prepared. On this night officers and soldiers of the National People's Army set out with artillery and tanks for the border to West Berlin.

As dawn broke on the morning of August 13, 1961, the soldiers of the NPA, together with members of the People's Police, the border police, and the members (Genossen) of the fighting groups erected an antifascist defense wall in Berlin. All the streets, subway stations, and squares leading to West Berlin were controlled by them. Thereby was the national border to West Berlin secure and reliably defended. Peace was saved. From this day on, the warmongers could not, as they had previously, disturb the reconstruction and peaceful life of our country. Our border soldiers stand guard over peace.[6]

The Wall is interrupted at eleven different points: eight checkpoints between East and West Berlin and three highway checkpoints, for those wishing to make the drive from West Berlin through the GDR to the "mainland." Checkpoints between the two cities vary according to whom they accommodate: some are for use by foreigners, others are only for West Berliners, and still others are reserved for citizens of the Federal Republic of Germany. All visitors, regardless of origin, must return to the West by midnight of the day of their visit. Until the fall of 1980, the minimum daily exchange rate for visitors to East Berlin, and elsewhere in the GDR, was DM 13 (about $7.00). In 1979, eight million West Germans and West Berliners took advantage of this affordable rate. Yet in 1980 the GDR government decided to double the exchange rate, which effectively reduced the number of visits by half without any appreciable loss of western currency. At that time Poland was experiencing internal upheaval, and the GDR had felt it necessary to somehow decrease its citizens' contacts with the West in an effort to ensure internal security.

Aside from the various checkpoints, there are other breaches in the Wall of an economic and political nature. In certain crucial respects the two cities are interdependent on one another. Commercial traffic flows back and forth on waterways, railroads, and highways. East Berlin takes care of much of West Berlin's garbage disposal. In turn, East Berlin requires hard western currency, and to that end operates Intershops where western luxury items can be purchased with western currency. And, like other Eastern Bloc countries, the GDR is very dependent on western bank loans. Still, there are enormous differences between these two cities of Berlin.

West Berlin

Depending on one's point of view, West Berlin is either "the last outpost of freedom" or "the showcase of capitalism." It is a gaudy yet sophisticated, crude yet intelligent city, full of contradictions of a geographical as well as a social nature. To the north of the city lies the small village of Lübars nestled up against the Wall, while in the working class districts of Wedding or Kreuzberg (where I met many of my informants) one experiences the intensely jarring noises and smells of hectic urban life. Farther to the south and west are the wealthier districts of Dahlem and Wilmersdorf.

West Berlin is an enormous city: thirty-two kilometers from north to south, and twenty-nine kilometers from west to east. Its twelve districts are interconnected by an efficient and sophisticated mass transport system. Two of the subway lines run beneath East Berlin, without stopping, and passengers become accustomed to the sight of armed GDR soldiers patrolling the dark, long-since-unused subway stations of that city. Aboveground are major highways; it is no accident that West Berlin is a "sister city" to Los Angeles. With its 1.9 million inhabitants (expected to level off at 1.7 million), the city is densely populated; yet what is most striking to the visitor is the number of parks, forests, and lakes within the city limits (proscribed by the Wall itself). Thirty percent of the city is kept clear by zoning laws, and so, in spite of the potential claustrophobia of a town without a "hinterland," there are certain possibilities for "escape" —to parks like Tiergarten or Grunewald.

West Berlin is a city reeling in possibility. Its cultural offerings are endless—film festivals, music festivals, a renowned symphony and opera company, several major theater companies—made possible by the city's culture budget, which allocates 315 million marks a year to cover just about everything happening in the city.[7] It is a city where culture gets consumed at a rapid rate, like the expensive delicacies on display at the famous Kaufhaus des Westens (KaDeWe). In addition to the "official" and unofficial culture, the city is home for two excellent universities: the Free University and the Technical University, along with 185 research institutes of one kind or another.

Yet what distinguishes West Berlin is its location and its political status. The city lies approximately 140 kilometers inside the German Democratic Republic, not far from the Polish-GDR border. It is linked to the West by three major highways, six rail lines, and three air corridors. In spite of the city's isolation, travel to and from West Berlin has become considerably easier since the signing of the Quadripartite Agreement in 1971 and the subsequent ratification of a treaty between the two German states in 1972. Both agreements were concerned primarily with the question of transit to and from West Berlin, as well as visits from the West to relatives in the East. As a result, children and their families today can drive from their city of West Berlin to the Federal Republic of Germany with relative freedom from unnecessary delays.

In order to further diminish the distance between this city and its nation, the Federal Republic subsidizes flights to and from West Berlin. Yet such support does not stop there. To attract individuals and business to this "outpost" city, the government has offered a variety of inducements, at a cost of almost 10 billion deutsche marks a year in direct subsidy, and billions more in indirect subsidies like tax breaks and bonuses and special business credits.[8] These efforts have had some success, although demographic figures are still wildly askew: 30 percent of the population is over sixty-five and another 30 percent is under twenty-six.

Although West Berlin has been declared a federal state of the FRG, it continues to be administered by the three western Allies, and is divided into three corresponding sectors. Although they rarely intervene in local political decisions, the "Besatzungsmächte," or occupying forces, are entitled to final say in any decision of major significance. Should the residents of the city lose sight of the presence of twelve thousand Allied troops (among them seven thousand Americans), they can witness the annual display of Allied military strength that occurs on the "Tag der Allierten," or Allied Day, on May 15. On this day, crowds (grown smaller over the years) line the Street of the 17th of June,* which runs through the Tiergarten, stopping at the Wall and the Brandenburg Gate. Here the Allies put on a military parade that rivals those of the neighboring city of East Berlin, putting aside any doubts West Berliners might have as to who is ultimately in charge of their city.

As residents of an occupied city, West Berliners are unable to participate directly in national elections, nor are they required to serve in the military forces of the FRG. This has a very clear effect on the social fabric of the city, as thousands of young people from the "mainland" settle in West Berlin to avoid military conscription. Along with them come a great number of social "misfits." The city, as in the past, continues to be renowned for its particular brand of tolerance and thus is a magnet of sorts for young people of a variety of political, social, and personal convictions—a fact not unrelated to the incidence of street demonstrations so familiar to children of this city. One newspaper reported that there were 357 violent "demos" in West Berlin between June 1981 and June 1982.[9]

Although the protesters were varied and their aims diverse, they often started out in support of the "Hausbesetzer," house squatters intent on occupying abandoned houses and fixing them up for occupancy. They are trying to put a stop to the policy of speculators who buy up apartment houses in a city always short of cheap and adequate housing, leaving them empty until their value appreciates. It is an issue that many of the working class children I came to know respond to, owing to their own families' difficulties in finding acceptable living quarters. Other young people demonstrated against the U.S. plans to station new missiles on West German soil, prompting young children to reconsider their own ambivalent feelings toward the United States. Yet regardless of the particular aims of these numerous demonstrations, many of them degenerated into violent street battles with police—frightening displays of anarchy to children often caught up in them.

Aside from these daily demonstrations, another significant fact of West Berlin life is the visible presence of foreign guest workers (Gastarbeiter). As with the rest of the Federal Republic, West Berlin has attracted a great number of foreigners over the past decade, come to do the "dirty work" of

*Named in memory of that day, in 1953, when East German workers revolted against excessively high work norms.

a prosperous West Germany. Currently, the city of West Berlin is home to 230,000 "Gastarbeiter" and their families. Of those, approximately 120,000 are Turkish peasants from Anatolia, making this the fourth largest Turkish city in the world.[10] Kreuzberg, adjoining the Wall, and a decidedly working class area, has come to be called "Little Istanbul," while the subway line traversing the city east to west is frequently referred to as the "Orient Express." It is this last group that receives the brunt of growing German "Ausländerfeindlichkeit" (hatred of foreigners), which appears to be related to the steady decline of the once booming German economy. In certain districts of the city, primarily working class quarters, the presence of Turks is striking—and much on the minds of the children with whom I spoke.

West Berlin is a city of paradoxes; and children are left trying to sort out their impressions of all that goes on within their city's limits, as well as that which goes on right next door, to the other side of that wall for which their city has become renowned.

East Berlin

Unlike West Berlin, East Berlin does not consider itself an occupied city; rather it is the capital city of this German state of seventeen million citizens. Highway signs to the city read "Berlin—Hauptstadt der DDR" (Berlin—Capital of the GDR), and wherever the word *Berlin* is used, it is quickly linked with that latter phrase. A sure sign of a visitor's origins is whether or not he prefaces the name of the city with "East." This fact is in violation of postwar agreements between the four Powers pertaining to the status of the divided city: neither East nor West Berlin was to be fully integrated into its respective nation. Because of this, the city is not recognized as a state capital by the West Germans or the Americans. The Americans call their embassy in East Berlin an embassy *to*, not *in* the GDR. And officially in West Germany, the GDR is not a foreign state; they refer to their embassy in East Berlin as a "ständige Vertretung" (a permanent mission), and their ambassador is a "Missionchef."

Because of its position as the "Hauptstadt" of the GDR, this city of 1.1 million is "occupied" by East German troops, while the approximately 400,000 Russian soldiers in the GDR keep out of sight in the countryside.[11] The East German soldiers, members of the "Volksarmee," are highly visible—distinguished by their Prussian uniforms and goose step. During the changing of the guard at the Monument to the Victims of Fascism and

Militarism on the broad Unter den Linden, one is forcefully reminded of a military tradition that supposedly ended with the bombing of Berlin. It is a peculiar irony in view of GDR efforts to dissociate its people and traditions from its predecessor, the Third Reich.

Although East Berlin, like its other half, is a rebuilt city, the planners have made efforts to restore certain historic sections—particularly along the once famous Unter den Linden. This broad avenue, once popular for wedding processions, had previously run through the heart of Berlin. It was one reason Berlin had been considered among the most beautiful cities of Europe. Today it has been severely truncated by the Wall, and now runs from the Brandenburg Gate down to Alexanderplatz, a broad public expanse dominated by the television tower. Along this stretch—the focal point for most tourists—restored historic landmarks rise between the embassies of various socialist nations. Walking from the Brandenburg Gate, one passes Humboldt University, the Deutsche Oper (opera), and the impressive Museum Island, dominated by the Pergamon Museum— filled with Middle Eastern riches that were the yield of Germany's heyday in archaeology.

On this walk one also passes the statue of Frederick the Great (leader of Prussia from 1740 to 1786), restored along Unter den Linden in 1980. It had been dismantled in 1950 as a symbol of Prussian nationalism and militarism. Yet on the occasion of its return to public view, Frederick was described in the *Junge Welt*, a newspaper of the Young Communist League, as "a great and talented military commander who was the victor in four wars, a unique feat in Prussian history."[12] The return of the statue is indicative of two significant facts about the German Democratic Republic: first, the nation's leaders are looking to answer the need for more "national identification in a country considered artificial and nonpermanent by its own citizens";[13] and second, it is in line with the increased militarization of the society, especially of the education of the young. During the spring of 1982, West German newspapers reported on the "Feindbild" (enemy picture) in the GDR, saying that East Berlin wanted to develop a "stable enemy consciousness" that would make citizens immune to the "demoralizing" influence of the West.[14]

This emphasis on the political can be seen throughout East Berlin. Although the city lacks the advertising of the West, it nonetheless possesses its own color—mostly shades of red—derived from the ubiquitous political advertising. Citizens are constantly reminded, by placards and banners, of the priorities of socialism, the dangers of fascism, and the special friendship between the GDR and the Soviet Union. This brand of propaganda is exaggerated in the capital city by virtue of East Berlin's proximity to the West. Not only is the city visited by millions of westerners each year, it is also the recipient of West German television signals, and so must work especially hard at countering the undermining influence of capitalism. This is done not only through blatant propaganda, but through government efforts to make the city a "showcase of socialism." Hence, living conditions are markedly better here; salaries are higher and prices lower than in the rest of the nation. Although there are still shortages and frequent lines for especially sought after goods, life is not quite so difficult in this regard. Because of its special privileges, the city is often spoken of with resentment elsewhere in the GDR. And by its own residents the city is often mocked for its preponderance of bureaucrats and "Filz," or corruption. They sometimes refer to their city as "Volvograd," in reference to the automobile of choice of most government officials—in a nation where the average working person must wait seven years for an East German car.

In certain important respects East Berlin has made remarkable gains since the war. Housing continues to go up at a rapid rate, and several areas of the city are now dominated by high-rise apartment houses. Although the government has done an impressive job of closing the gap between available housing and individual need, the wait for an apartment can still exceed seven years. Meanwhile, families double up; young people and their spouses stay on with parents, until something better can be found. In contrast to the numerous "neubau" areas, where most of those new apartments will be leased, there are still districts that show the scars of war, and are reminiscent of the Berlin that existed more than half a century ago. Like those of West Berlin, the eight districts of East Berlin offer a diverse urban landscape—from the pastoral scene of the "village" of Rosenthal to the inner-city grittiness of Prenzlauer Berg. It is districts like the latter that were evoked by the novelist Alfred Döblin, and there that one sees the sharp difference between East and West Berlin. The visitor to these working class districts of East Berlin, especially in the soft glow of their evening streetlamps, experiences an "older," less hectic Berlin—a respite from the frenzy of the West.

Yet the city, and nation, wage their unique struggles. During my stay, while the government was stepping up the militarization of the nation (partly in response to events in Poland), the church-affiliated peace movement was growing and becoming articulate. Young people had been enrolling in the Lutheran church at an increasing rate, and in February

1982, five thousand of them assembled in Dresden's Church of the Cross for a "peace forum." Later that spring the church issued a statement supporting young East Germans who refused military service, saying that they were "expressing pro-disarmament and not anti-state sentiments."[15] Although not all children were taken with the church's message, they were witness to the possibility of challenging the state, and could see that struggle become organized, not simply expressed in the angry but muted mutterings of parents or friends.

East Berlin is a city where the life of the nation gets writ large. Here children are in the best position to derive the benefits of their system, as well as observe its contradictions and particular failings. In addition, they can clearly see the various opponents to the state—the church from within, and the West (visitors and television) from the other side of the Wall. Like West Berlin, the city derives much of its significance (in reality and in the minds of children) from its relationship with its neighbor "over there."

3 | Method

In order for a particular methodology to be useful it should fulfill at least three conditions: it must effectively address the research question(s); it must conform to the requirements (political, social) of the field; and it must be sensitive to specific ethical dilemmas which inevitably arise in the course of such work. In the case of my Berlin work those conditions were best met through the use of direct observation in "the field"[1] along with the "clinical" method described by Erik Erikson in *Childhood and Society*.[2] The researcher must listen not only to the words of his informants, but also must pay close attention to the richly varied "background noise" of their lives. Their words must be viewed within a context—familial, social, and political. I not only observed; I became involved directly in the lives of the children I came to know. The clinical method to which I refer allows one to explore the process by which people create meaning—how they organize and interpret the wildly assorted "data" of their daily lives. In the office such a method relies on "a core of disciplined subjectivity in both patient and analyst, which it is neither desirable nor possible to replace altogether with seemingly more objective methods—methods which originate, as it were, in the machine tooling of other kinds of work."[3] I would argue that the same holds true in the field.

I have sought to understand how children perceive and make sense of the especially striking political climate of East and West Berlin. In so doing, I have tried to document the complexity of this area of their life—a task that required methodological tools that enabled me to look closely and carefully not only at individual children but also at the dramatic political and social setting in which they live their lives. This is a study about the relationship between the child and his nation, yet one that was conducted in a field not especially amenable to the efforts of the researcher. As I shall illustrate, political conditions in East Berlin are such that methodological tools that might be quite helpful and available in West Berlin (the use of questionnaires, tape-recorded interviews, and other research parapher-nalia) are out of the question. Because of the great discrepancy in "research hospitality" of both cities, it soon became clear to me that although I would approach similar issues with children on both sides of the Wall, my means of so doing would have to differ substantially, as would my manner of establishing a sample of children.

West Berlin, a lively intellectual center as well as a city embracing west-ern democratic values, is relatively open to the sort of probing my research entailed. East Berlin, on the other hand, is decidedly not. Here is a political system extremely averse to western scrutiny, where children are perceived as the "new generation of socialism"; hence, visits with westerners, for whatever reasons, are officially discouraged. This is not to say that I could not speak with children, but that I was forced down back alleys and through back doors (literally as well as figuratively) to learn things that are readily accessible in the West.

Such disparate research conditions prevented me from finding children in both cities who shared similar backgrounds (most likely an impossible task on account of the very different ideological worlds—hence, social, cultural, and economic reality—these children occupy). I did manage, however, to speak with boys and girls in East and West Berlin of ten to twelve years old. These variables alone—sex and age—may be the only clear points of similarity between the groups of children.

In West Berlin I visited elementary schools in several of the twelve dis-tricts that make up the city. I met with fifth and sixth graders and their teachers. Through general conversation with these children (they often taking the lead), I acquired a broad sense of their interests and concerns. I would then go on to inquire more specifically as to their feelings in regard to certain political issues, beginning with the Berlin Wall. While continu-ing these larger class discussions, I came to know a smaller group of eight children more intimately. I would meet with these youngsters twice a month at least. Usually I would spend that time with individual children, although I also held several group meetings. These meetings lasted any-where from one hour to the whole day. Although the children reflected the socioeconomic range to be found in West Berlin, I must stress that they are not intended as spokesmen for their peers; rather, they speak for themselves. Yet in so doing, they reveal over time certain shared considerations and preoccupations that have become the substance of this study.

In East Berlin it was impossible to visit elementary schools. And even if it were possible to speak with children in the classroom, the pressure they feel to voice officially held dogma and to suppress all conflicting personal feelings is so strong as to make this means of approach somewhat useless. Children under any circumstances, in any political system, will not quickly voice their opinions for the benefit of an outsider; there are all sorts of pressures that work against that. However, in East German schools, the consequences for publicly voicing opinions contrary to the "party line" are serious and feared. Hence, I adopted other means of locating and speaking with children in this country that actively (and fairly effectively) discourages just that.

First, there are individuals in West Berlin who have relatives in the East. I visited these families, and as a certain degree of trust and friendliness was established, they would in turn introduce me to friends of theirs. Secondly, the Lutheran church in East Germany is the strongest voice of opposition to the government and is increasingly articulate in its criticism of official policies. It is fast becoming a refuge for those people no longer satisfied with things as they are, and it is a place where individuals can fairly freely voice opinions contrary to those demanded of them by various government representatives (politicians, teachers, youth group leaders). And the church organizes children's groups, which I was invited to attend. Here I met various children, and through them, met others who were not members. The role of the church in the child's political and moral development is significant, and will be addressed at a later point.

Finally, I found it necessary to make contacts with children in parks and on the streets. Obviously such encounters were hit or miss; but in a political landscape such as East Germany, these casual, unofficial contacts were far and away safer for me as an observer, as well as for the children and families with whom I spoke. Although I spoke at least once with a large number of children, I was able to speak with only six on a regular basis. By regular, I mean once a week at best, twice a month at least. The circumstances of these meetings were similar to those I held with West Berlin children.

During my year-long stay in both cities I gathered information in a variety of ways. I conducted numerous open-ended interviews with the children. These interviews inevitably covered a good deal of territory, although my abiding interest lay in children's feelings toward their political world. By raising specific questions, as well as allowing children to make their own unsolicited comments and observations, I feel that I was able, over time, to better understand how these young people see themselves vis-à-vis their particular political environments.

I have tried at all points to avoid excessive abstraction in the hope of witnessing and recording the lives of these children as faithfully as possible. Therefore, in addition to the interviews, I spent time with children, individually and in groups, at home as well as out and about. By such direct observation of and participation (to varying degrees) in their everyday lives, I feel I was in a unique position to view their interview comments within the larger context of their lives.

I gathered drawings from these children. As a clinical tool, and as a research tool, a child's drawing (or series of drawings) is often very helpful in enabling the clinician or researcher to better understand that child's concerns that he may not address verbally.[4] Often I would ask children to draw anything at all; choice of subject was left to their own discretion. And sometimes I would provide the subject. The value of a drawing for the researcher often depends on its value for a youngster. Some children who were fairly relaxed and articulate speakers found drawings "childish" and put little effort into them. Others, their imaginations given free rein in the artistic process, poured forth a wealth of material, using color and form vividly. Occasionally a drawing became a springboard for discussion, in fact, revealed—to the child himself—certain attitudes and feelings that until that moment may well have remained vague, unarticulated.

My experience with Torsten (see East Berlin case study, chapter 5) is a good example. I came to know this ten-year-old boy in the roundabout fashion with which I made the acquaintance of all these East Berlin children. His family has friends in West Berlin; and they suggested I meet with Torsten. I was able to meet with the boy after a somewhat awkward introduction to his parents. As with most parents in East Berlin, they felt a distinct mix of generosity and strong suspicion. It was the slow unfolding of months that helped minimize that doubt and mistrust. Still, a certain unease remained: for even if I was to be trusted, there was always a political risk entailed in becoming too friendly with westerners. I enjoyed meeting with Torsten; he was playful and relaxed, and quite willing to give a somewhat nervous and excessively curious stranger the benefit of the doubt. Nonetheless, we eventually reached what might be called an impasse: I felt uneasy and unsure as to how to proceed; and he was not quite sure what I was up to. At this point I requested that Torsten draw me a picture of "something I should know about your country" (desperation as mother of methodology). He quickly, to my great relief, made a stark representation of the Berlin Wall, out of which flowed a remarkably detailed personal response to that reality and what it represents for him. Somehow that drawing (or the act of drawing) enabled Torsten to tap into feelings of his that were kept separate from the opinions he often felt required to give me (and which he no doubt, to some degree, held as well).

In addition to the direct work I did with children, I also spoke with parents, siblings, and other family members. Such conversations were extremely valuable, aiding in my fuller appreciation of certain children. As well, I spoke with teachers, who not only have insights into the behavior of specific children, but are responsible for educating children to become members of a particular political system.

Clearly, the work I have conducted is grounded in subjectivity—from my manner of choosing children to the way in which I conducted our various conversations. As I will continue to try to make clear, the peculiar situation in which I found myself made a reasonably controlled study impossible. Yet such subjectivity may offer up insights not accessible by other means.

I had far fewer problems conducting this research in West Berlin. Occasionally I was denied access to children in particular schools on account of the political persuasion of one or another headmaster. Those who were more conservative were often wary of outsiders—especially when they were university students interested in speaking with children about political issues. Berlin is a volatile city, politically and socially. Hence, school administrators were often uneasy at the prospect of allowing a stranger to initiate politically oriented discussions with children. Despite these fears, I found that most children with whom I spoke were hardly in need of an outsider to stimulate an interest in local politics (though, to be sure, the tone and direction of their talk was undoubtedly influenced by my presence). They were all too aware of the two pressing political and social issues plaguing West Berlin: "Hausbesetzer" and the "Gastarbeiter." These concerns and the city's relation to East Berlin were often ready sources of conversation.

Despite resistance in certain schools, I was able to pursue my inquiry relatively unhindered. I was strongly encouraged in some schools, such as the Möwensee Grundschule in Wedding, where the headmaster was not only instrumental in arranging classroom visits but was generously forthcoming with his own views. During that first meeting he offered the following observation: "Children here don't think about the Wall; nor do they concern themselves with life in the East. They have grown up here and are accustomed to the strange life this city offers them. They are like children everywhere; their neighborhood is their world." I heard this repeatedly expressed by adults, and in a sense it is true. Certainly not all children, when asked what this visitor should know about their city, immediately made mention of the Wall. In West Berlin, children frequently reeled off a list of "Sehenswürdigkeiten" (worthwhile tourist sites)—the "Funkturm" (radio tower), Tiergarten, the EEC Congress Hall, Reichstag, Gedächtniskirche (Kaiser Wilhelm Memorial Church on Kurfürstendamm), the Brandenburger Tor, the Olympiastadium—which rarely included the Berlin Wall. And in East Berlin, young people took advantage of the question to explain the nature of life in the GDR—in both positive and negative terms, without direct reference to the Wall.

Yet as time went on, I saw that these initial responses in no way contradicted the significance of the Wall. For many children it had become such a part of their lives, and had for so long defined the parameters (political, geographical, and psychological) of their lives that it no longer came immediately to mind. As twelve-year-old Klaus said, "It is like a tree in the playground. At first you keep wishing it wasn't there; it's always getting in the way. But then you get used to it and stop noticing it altogether." Also, children in West Berlin wanted to give this outsider a favorable impression of their city, to show off those aspects of their life that they felt some pride in and derived some pleasure from. On several occasions, when I would ask whether the Wall should be included in that list of "Sehenswürdigkeiten," I was told: "Oh, that's not something good about the city. You don't really want to see that; it's ugly. Tiergarten is so much nicer, and you can really enjoy yourself there." Children in East Berlin had other reasons, rooted in fear and a reasonable amount of distrust, for not wanting to address so touchy a subject too quickly. But during just such moments as these, when children tried to steer me in a direction away from the Wall, one less painful and confusing, they would begin to give voice to their own lengthy and complicated opinions on the subject. Of course, these opinions rarely were delivered in one sitting; nor were they always consistent. Acquiring an understanding of the political world, and establishing one's personal involvement with that world, is a long process; and I found myself quite in the center of it with these children.

It was in the Möwensee Grundschule that I made my first and most rewarding contacts with children; and here where I learned how revealing direct observation can be, especially when one is navigating in strange territory. The first such occasion was a class trip to the northern West German territory of Schlesswig-Holstein, a low-lying lake district dominated by a large brooding sky. Such class trips to West Germany are built into the West Berlin curriculum; they serve to remind children that their city is indeed isolated within East Germany, but that it is also politically linked with the Federal Republic of Germany. As well, all Berliners value those opportunities to flee the city and its peculiar brand of malaise, "Mauerkrankheit," and children are no exception.

I was to spend ten days with thirty children and their teachers in the small village of Bosau, not far from the port city of Lübeck. During that brief time I observed much, heard much in ways that would have been impossible had I insisted on interviewing children within the confines of their school. We were to travel by bus, which entails a three-hour crossing of East Germany. One simply cannot appreciate the isolation of West Berlin (or the significance that holds for many people) by flying into the city. By so doing, one avoids the harsh reminders of the city's geographical predicament—specifically the border crossings.

It was at just such a crossing that I got my first glimpse of how that actuality affects young children, some of whom have made the trip several times by the age of twelve. One can never be sure just how long or how difficult one of the crossings will be. Up until 1971 and the signing of the Quadripartite Agreement (in which the East guaranteed Westerners unrestricted access to West Berlin and gave West Berliners thirty days a year in which to visit friends and relatives in the East in exchange for western acknowledgment of the legitimacy of the German Democratic Republic), such crossings remained a painful, infuriating process. Since that time they go considerably smoother, although that still depends on the amount of traffic fleeing the city, as well as on the disposition of particular GDR border guards. Although they are always methodical, they can give new meaning to that word on certain days. The West Berliner behind the wheel can only wait, and mutter under his breath.

On this particular October day there was relatively little traffic. The children had been excited and noisy as the bus made its way through several districts of Berlin: Wedding, Charlottenburg, Spandau. Many of these children come from working class families, and any occasion to leave the city is extremely welcome. The signs indicating our approach to the border went largely ignored as the children continued their playful banter. Suddenly we were there; the bus pulled up to a spot indicated by several waving GDR guards. Just as abruptly, the children fell silent and turned their eyes, ears, and thoughts to the scene going on about them.

It was difficult to determine whether the cause for this sudden cessation of activity was fear, awe, curiosity, or a knowledge (born from experience) that the crossing always goes more quickly when one remains quiet and polite. I soon came to see that all of these responses commingled in the minds of these children. In addition, there was anger and defiance, none of which was openly expressed until the bus was safely in West Germany some three hours later. Yet, as we waited, the children wanted to let me know what we were contending with. "You can't call them 'Ostschweine' (east pigs) here, or else they'll just pull you off the bus and throw you in jail"; or, "they hate us, and so we hate them." These comments were interrupted by the arrival on the bus of one of the guards. Carefully making his way down the aisle, he proceeded to match up documents with the various kids. They in turn followed him with their gaze, clearly uncertain as to what to expect; he was a forceful, unforgettable reminder of those larger political realities that children are often presumed to ignore. In this space of time—a bus ride from the heart of West Berlin to a border checkpoint, a total of an hour perhaps—these children had faced a few hard facts about power and politics: their city is surrounded by an "enemy"; although they remain safe within their own territory, the borders to that safety are clearly demarcated.

After this border delay, the bus resumed its trek, now inside the GDR. The children visibly relaxed, though it was not until they reached West German soil that they cheered ("It's better here than 'over there' "), and let go with a brief frenzy their pent-up energies that had been fueled by a host of confused feelings aroused during that three-hour journey through "enemy" territory. This particular highway linking West Berlin with the FRG is old and poorly maintained. Unlike the newer transit routes, it wends its way through various East German towns and villages, affording the traveler a brief, superficial glimpse of socialist life. Responses from the children on the bus varied: "Look at those houses—so dirty"; "It's so old-looking there; everything is falling apart"; or, "They don't live as well here as we do in the West." Perhaps because the evidence for assurance and optimism cannot be located so readily in the towns and cities of the GDR, the government there has posted large, colorful signs—everywhere—extolling the virtues of socialism. These West Berlin children took note of them and registered their zealous message, which they slowly mulled over and examined. Of course, such political advertising was often glibly dismissed; but, as I would find out later, such glibness could also be a cover for uncertainty and confusion. Children were least inclined to be reflective during that brief span of time within a hostile nation, and it was not until we had settled down in Bosau, and later in West Berlin, that they felt secure enough to qualify some of their earlier statements.

I write about this experience because it reveals the value of direct observation of these children's lives, especially when used in collaboration with more in-depth conversations. To know what it is children are responding to, and to witness their response, can be very illuminating, and serves as a jumping-off point for later discussion: Why did you cheer when we got through the border? Why are those soldiers there? How is the GDR different from the FRG? There was no substitute for such an approach as a means of understanding the various dramas in which these children participate.

Such was my introduction to one group of children. There were, among these, several with whom I spoke more frequently. I came to know individual children in various ways: Matthias enjoyed the outdoors, which is where—in some of Berlin's lovely parks—our conversations took place; Klaus, with a keen interest in history, often met me at one of the several museums that grace the city; and Claudine, one of the few children from this particular school with an intact, apparently happy family, was content to meet me at her home. In other words, the conditions under which I met with various children varied considerably according to their interest, as well as to mine.

In East Berlin there is no way that a visitor from the West can freely visit schools and speak candidly with children. As the mother of one of my young informants told me, "They'll say they'll help you, but they'll only show you what they want you to see. And if you *do* visit a school, you can be sure they'll be well prepared for your visit. Everything is under control here." Nevertheless, I found myself one fall day walking into the "Haus des Lehrers" (Education Ministry), a bland office building along Alexanderplatz, the renovated heart of East Berlin. I was introduced to two officials in charge of foreign visitors and gave a (somewhat veiled) account of my intentions. I was an educator from the United States, I said, interested in socialist educational practices, with hopes of visiting elementary schools and talking with children. I was treated cordially, and in fact was soon engaged in a lengthy discussion of German literature. As that wound down, I was told to return in two weeks in order to meet yet another official who would lead me on a tour of schools. Yet no mention was made of schools during that subsequent visit, until I brought it up. The response was once again to return in two weeks' time. On that third visit I was driven around the city and given a fine lunch at a lakeside cafe on the southeast perimeter of the city. Afterward we (a rather friendly, depressed bureaucrat and myself) visited the "Pionierpalast" (Pioneer Palace), a massive youth center complete with olympic-size pool, numerous sports facilities, simulated space flight centers, and a host of "activities" rooms—the pride of East German officialdom. Still no school visit. I began to see just how insistently these officials intended to stage an elaborate runaround without ever uttering the word "no."

During this period I had continued to wander around the city well off the beaten tourist track, down the still war-torn, scarred side streets, or into the "neubau" (newly built) high-rise districts such as Marzahn. Here in "the field" I despaired of making contacts, and knew only one thing for certain: that I was increasingly tired and in need of a better pair of shoes. It was during one of these low moments that I happened to stumble onto Bergstrasse, a street several blocks long, lined with crumbling five-story apartment houses that somehow had been spared during the final days of the war, when so much of Berlin raged in fire and collapse. I was struck by the peaceful, run-down quality of that scene: geraniums blooming in numerous narrow windows, heavy-set Prussian women leaning out to converse with one another, young children racing along the street. I was so close to it all, yet how to break into such a community? As I made my way by an old, dilapidated, though still operating coal shop, two thirteen-year-old boys sitting on a stoop spied me and asked for a cigarette. My western origins were clear to them: jeans, "Rücksack," shoes, and my bearing were all clear signals. I stopped, explained that I was an American, and watched an absolutely shocked and delighted expression come over their faces. They had never met an American, and soon were introducing me to other children on the street, almost as though I was their "find." Such a strange, inauspicious beginning was, for me, the start of a year of fieldwork. Bergstrasse became my home base of sorts, although I came to know children throughout the city.

Yet East Berlin consistently remained a serious challenge to my investigative efforts. In this city, practical considerations are firmly wedded to ethical ones: I was continually forced to ask not only whether a particular approach would be feasible, but I also had to consider whether I was ever putting individual children or their families at risk. Although ethical considerations must be confronted in all fieldwork, the consequences for ignoring them can be especially serious in East Berlin. Earlier I mentioned the risks individuals run if they persist in maintaining personal contact with westerners. Consequences for "improper" behavior are meted out rather arbitrarily and include visits from the police, or Stasi (Staatsicherheitsdienst, or National Security Apparatus), which range from annoying to extremely uncomfortable. As well, children may begin to receive poorer marks in school if it is felt they are paying too little attention to socialist concerns. I have heard stories of the downward slide of children precipitated by behavior or voiced opinions deemed "inappropriate" for a socialist mentality. Because of these risks, many parents forbade their children to speak with me.

My encounter with the mother of a young boy I had met is very revealing in this regard. I had met eleven-year-old Hans through a friend of his, Torsten (about whom I have already spoken). Hans was delighted to meet an "Ami" (American) and eagerly anticipated my visits to his neighborhood (a mixed community of professionals and skilled workers on the northeastern edge of the city). Soon after I met Hans, I decided to meet with his parents in order to be sure they approved of my meetings with their son. One brisk winter day I arrived at his house, where I was greeted somewhat coolly by his mother. She invited me into their apartment, remarkable for its spaciousness, high ceilings, large French windows overlooking a deep backyard, genuine Persian rugs, books lining the walls—altogether very comfortable, and an indication of the relatively high status Hans's family enjoys. It was a family with more to lose, in fact, than the less well-off families I had come to know elsewhere in East Berlin.

After a few pleasantries this woman set out to teach me an important lesson in the nature of the relationship between the child, the family, and the state. "I was quite surprised when Hans told us about you. We had heard nothing at all about you until you called. I asked him who you were and what you talked about. You see, he never tells us anything; he's a very quiet child. He said you told him stories about where you've been in the world; that you once met a real cowboy, and that you have a backpack that he says he could fit into and so go to America with you. He just doesn't understand it yet, why he can't travel around the way you can. For a child his age it's confusing.

But let me tell you a few things about Hans, so you understand better. He hasn't had it easy. I was divorced when he began going to school. We were living in another part of Berlin then. I'm not sure how upset Hans was by the divorce, as his father never really paid much attention to him anyhow. But he began having trouble in school. In the first grade . . . well, he was causing trouble; but the teacher never understood him at all. And didn't try to. She blamed him for everything, and kept him back. He had no friends, and I think he was a very lonely child.

So we moved here, and it seemed to get better. His teacher is a lively type and has no prejudice toward Hans. He seems to be doing better in school, and has a few friends. But I still worry about him because he's so easily influenced and doesn't really know what he thinks. So I worry about your effect on him, if you see what I mean. Well, that's some kind of personal explanation of why I think you shouldn't see him.

But there are political reasons, too. I don't want you to think we're oppressed here; it's not so obvious as that. But here everything is political, and children haven't learned, by the time they're Hans's age, not to say certain things. I worry about what will happen if it gets around that Hans sees you. It could affect his school situation, and even his job later on. Look, I'm not in favor of this country. My husband is not in the Party, and I left it several years ago. But we know how this system works, and I don't want Hans to suffer from it.

We have a group called "Eltern Aktive" [Parents Council], which meets once a month or so and decides what the children will do on class trips and and how certain holidays will be celebrated. But of course they are always concerned with the political education of the children; and they may think, if they hear of this, that you're trying to turn Hans toward the church. And you must know that the peace movement has made the church almost an enemy of the state; and we're not religious at all, and don't raise Hans to be. Or they may think you will try to turn him toward the "Konsumkultur" of the West. And he learns enough about that from television here. Why, my five-year-old son can spot a motorcycle all the way up the street and know what kind of Honda it is. The kids here are very aware of what's offered in the West—especially when it comes to cars and motorcycles. But too much of that influence is bad; children can't really understand it.

Even if you don't plan to have talks about political matters with Hans, it will be seen that way here. Politics is everywhere. You must know our society well enough by now. So, I am afraid for all these reasons that you must not see Hans again.

It is a statement that clearly reveals the manner in which the explicitly personal is bound up with the political. Not all parents managed to so precisely define their just cause for misgivings, and for that reason I was grateful to Hans's mother. Certainly her words were a strong reminder of how important it is to confer with parents before speaking with children, to realize that youngsters might indeed be unaware of the risks involved, or willing to disregard those risks. (I must add, however, that I found many children who, by the age of ten, were well aware of what they could and could not say in school, or beyond the ears of a trusted few.)

Yet what should the investigator interested in speaking with children do when he is made aware of the precarious, if not downright dangerous position in which his presence thrusts certain individuals? Clearly the safety of "informants" must be his first consideration; but how does one assure that safety when the various dangers are never entirely discernible? I struggled along with this issue, never to my complete satisfaction. I guaranteed the anonymity of all those with whom I spoke. I rarely took notes while in East Berlin, but waited until my return in the evening to West Berlin. Interviews were not tape-recorded; all names have been changed in any writing about that time and place. In fact, I have written about all these children in both cities in such a way that none of them can be identified. Yet while I was there, I was never fully satisfied with my efforts at protectiveness.

I recall a walk with Jörg, a fourteen-year-old boy living in a working class neighborhood of the Mitte district (what was once the center of a unified Berlin). On this particular day we had wandered into a cemetery not far from his house. Unknown to me, the far end of this cemetery touched on the inner wall of the border between East and West Berlin. As with most young people in the East, Jörg is very perceptive of his immediate surroundings, and he spotted the police officer as soon as he entered the cemetery behind us. Not only spotted him, but knew instantly that he was there on our account. The officer waited at the entrance and requested our identification as we were leaving. (By the age of fourteen, all East German individuals must carry a "Personalausweis," an identity card providing certain facts of their existence: name, address, occupation.) As poor luck would have it, Jörg had lost his Ausweis a few days earlier. Immediately my name and passport number were noted in a small black book, alongside the names of other like transgressors. For Jörg, the problem was much more serious. It simply looks bad, suspicious, to be so close to the border, especially in the presence of an American. And then to have no identification. . . . After several minutes of insistent interrogation, and the arrival of three or four more policemen, I was released, while Jörg was whisked off to the local precinct house for further questioning. He was released only at the insistence of his mother, who had found his ID and hurried off, in anger and fear, to secure her son.

I later learned that only people with relatives buried in that particular cemetery are allowed to visit; this is a "Grenzgebiet" (border zone) and generally off limits. I am sure Jörg knew this, yet for reasons of his own either forgot or chose to ignore that knowledge. At the time I felt he simply did not want to acknowledge such restrictions on his freedom. Yet, in assuming liberties that he in fact does not enjoy, he not only faces immediate censure but runs the very real risk of later employment difficulties. It does not take much to set off such a chain of deleterious consequences. I was left wondering then, and I wonder now, to what degree any outsider, relying on a degree of political immunity, endangers the welfare of citizens not granted that same immunity.

At this point I should add that in the five years that have passed since I conducted this research I have been in touch with all of the children I knew, and I am satisfied that although my concerns for their well-being may have been well founded, none of these youngsters appears to have suffered on account of our acquaintance.

The two important issues that I have introduced—abiding concern for the safety of informants and the uninterrupted pursuit of my research interests—were highlighted at the juncture of East and West, the border crossings. As it turned out, these points along the Wall between the two Berlins exerted the most significant influence on the manner in which I carried out my work. As an American visitor to East Berlin, I had two possible points of entry into East Berlin: Checkpoint Charlie and Checkpoint Friedrichstrasse. For the most part I used the former—both on account of its proximity to my West Berlin residence and for the fact that security checks at this checkpoint were often less stringent than those at the larger Friedrichstrasse station, which accommodates West Berliners and FRG residents as well as non-German foreigners.

By "less stringent" I do not suggest by any means that security at Checkpoint Charlie was lax. Yet the smaller volume of daily visitors made for a less hectic tone to the whole crossing procedure and consequently a more relaxed attitude among several of the guards. Although using the same checkpoint so frequently invites suspicion, it also has the advantage of putting one on more familiar terms with particular guards. Over time, as I came to know the various border officials and their work shifts, there were some who became cordial, if not friendly—willing to banter for a brief moment or two; whereas others remained difficult and aloof. The point here is that I began to differentiate various guards, to learn on whom I could count to conduct a less rigorous search, or who would be sure to make my crossing as difficult and humiliating as possible. This all became extremely important on those occasions when I had to take certain research materials (such as children's drawings) back into West Berlin. Still, despite this caution, I was frequently surprised by sudden alterations in the guards' schedules.

I can best convey the significant impact of this checkpoint on the actual carrying-out of my research by giving an account of the place itself, along with the procedure one undergoes to visit or leave East Berlin. Checkpoint Charlie lies at the end of Friedrichstrasse, south of the still stunning Unter den Linden. It straddles the border between the Mitte district of East Berlin and the Kreuzberg district of West Berlin. On the approach from West Berlin the visitor to the East passes several sentry boxes manned by the West Berlin police and soldiers of the three Allied powers: the United States, England, France. Their role is presumably to keep an account of border crossings, as well as to make their presence visible to the East. The visitor need have nothing to do with them. He then proceeds thirty yards farther to the first gate between East and West. Here, the concrete Wall is interrupted by Friedrichstrasse and the whole checkpoint apparatus.

This particular checkpoint is accessible both to vehicles and pedestrians. When walking, the visitor waits outside this first gate until a buzzer signals the release of its lock. On stepping inside, he is immediately greeted by an East German soldier demanding his passport. Generally this is a perfunctory check, after which he is sent along a narrow corridor through an open shed. At the far end is a sign directing him to the left and to the second checkpoint. Here he joins other visitors in a corral of sorts and is asked to surrender his passport and wait. After a delay (which varies from five minutes to half an hour or more, depending on the flow of traffic and the degree to which individual passports are scrutinized), he is then ushered up to a window to collect his passport and pay a visa fee of five West German marks. Another buzzer is heard, a second gate opens, and the visitor heads into a small building where yet another check takes place. At this point a search may be conducted, though its thoroughness depends on several factors, among them the appearance of the visitor and the temperament of the soldier on duty. It is usually at this point that the visitor realizes that the West is now behind him—that different rules prevail here. When he passes this search, he proceeds to a cashier's window where he exchanges twenty-five West German marks for the same amount of East German currency (approximately thirteen U.S. dollars at that time). He then leaves the building and heads toward the outer gate, where he waits to be "controlled" once more, and to hear the by now familiar buzzer signaling the opening of the final gate, whereupon he steps into East Berlin. It is frequently a very trying procedure, a stark political lesson that reduces the visitor's initial confidence, making him especially aware of his status in a system heavily reliant on widespread surveillance. The whole procedure, save for money changing, is repeated on leaving the city.

Because of this unnerving display of German "Grundlichkeit" (something akin to "thoroughness," only more so), it is generally impossible to carry any research materials without fear of apprehension. As a rule, one is forbidden to bring any western "political" literature into East Berlin, but the interpretation of the word *political* is left up to the guard's discretion. One is also forbidden to bring certain items out of the East, though just what these were was made clear to me only after I had violated some rule. Occasionally I managed successfully to take certain children's drawings out of the city, relying on the fact that I was, after a few months, a "known quantity" and less subject to suspicion and search (a dubious assumption, I would later realize). Yet on one occasion, while bringing a batch of children's drawings out of East Berlin, I was searched, and the drawings found and confiscated. I was thoroughly questioned as to who these children were and how I knew them. I responded in my worst German, remained evasive, and was finally released and admonished never to "traffic" in children's drawings again. I decided soon thereafter to stop bringing such things back into the West. I feared both for myself and, more so, for the children with whom I spoke. Again, a reminder of how forcefully one's work is circumscribed by political reality.

Another element of cross-cultural research that requires comment is the researcher's language facility. Although I came to a certain fluency after several months in Berlin, I did indeed have difficulties during those first few months. Idioms often raced past my comprehension, and the subtleties of humor and metaphor were often lost on me. Certainly the issue of language was significant in the East, where direct references to politics or specific dissatisfactions are often abandoned in favor of the more oblique use of humor and metaphor. Sarcasm and irony are used in abundance here, and many individuals express their most intimate convictions in this manner. Yet a situation that on first glance appeared detrimental to the carrying out of my work offered distinct advantages. Children were extraordinarily patient, and eager to help me learn their language. My reliance on them often served to bond us in ways that would have been impossible had I come in as a fully independent investigator. These children of East and West Berlin became my cultural and linguistic interpreters, and they frequently spelled out ideas and feelings at greater length, and with a consequent enrichment of detail, in their efforts to assure my understanding. I never relied on "official" interpreters, as I found it necessary, especially in East Berlin, to maintain a fairly low profile. Finding young people familiar with English was difficult: in West Berlin they do not begin to learn that language (it is required) until the fifth grade; in East Berlin, Russian is the required second language, and no third language may be learned unless suitable grades are achieved in Russian.

I am aware that a native speaker would catch subtleties that I might never have been aware of. Yet I am also aware that an individual with a flawless command of German might be more distrusted in East Berlin than one who has certain struggles with that language. The chances of being a spy or an informer (for either side) are greater when one is fluent in German. That fact was not lost on the children with whom I spoke. My difficulties with the language were reassuring, strangely enough, to both children and adults. I believe I was more readily perceived as a relatively benign outsider, presumably of good intentions.

Yet an outsider I was, subject to the advantages and disadvantages that status entails. By virtue of my peculiar position, I was able to see what others more caught up in their own situation might fail to perceive. Not only was I granted a unique perspective; I also may have prompted those "insiders" to look afresh at their world and see it with new eyes. Certainly such an approach left this observer to wrestle with his own biases and subjectivity. How much did my very presence and background influence those with whom I spoke? How were my perceptions framed by *my* "political socialization"? Without a doubt, the fact of my nationality had a powerful effect on children in both East and West Berlin. Upon visiting West Berlin classrooms I was often greeted with much hand clapping and foot stomping; and at times I felt that the excitement my presence generated made it difficult for children to express a certain ambivalence they might feel toward the United States. Because I spent a year with many of these children, however, I feel that they became increasingly able to reveal the wider range of their feelings to me.

In East Berlin I was a rare exotic; America is a highly charged place for these children: the "enemy" according to official rhetoric, as well as the land of Walt Disney World and certain possibilities unavailable in the East. Children often had to struggle with their own mixed feelings toward me and what I stood for. For example, I cannot say that these children, or their parents, are *just* dissatisfied with their political system. For many, in fact, there are genuinely satisfying elements to that life. Nonetheless, it was apparent that my visits to these young people were not only a source of stimulation; they were also provocative, a display of a kind of freedom enjoyed in the West and forbidden in the East—freedom to travel. So, while children were eager to talk with the "Ami," they also resented what I had done and could do, and for the way in which my presence compelled them to somehow take stock of their own lives and particular unfulfilled yearnings.

Certainly the work I describe was complicated and difficult. Yet I suggest that there are good reasons (practical and ethical) for the use of a particular line of approach—direct and participant observation tethered to the "clinical method"—and that such an approach has its own intrinsic value as well. It is appropriate not only by virtue of the particular requirements of the field but because it enabled me to work on fairly intimate terms with children and to hear and see things that may have been inaccessible via other lines of inquiry.

4 | The Children of West Berlin

After the war, they—the Russians, Amis, French, and English—divided Germany and Berlin. Then they built the Wall. I'm not sure why. But it means we have to travel three or four hours through the GDR to get to *our* country. It's better here than there. When I travel through the GDR, I see them in their small cars, all crowded [laughter], while we go by in our Mercedes. They don't live as well as we do.

Also, they're less free over there than we are. They can't say what they like. If someone goes to Alex Platz and shouts "I hate the GDR," the Russians will grab him right away and throw him in jail. Here, if you shout you don't like the mayor, nobody bothers you. You can say what you like.

Over there they don't like us. Children have to all go out and greet Honecker when he visits, and he tells them we're all rotten people here—fascists who only want war. We don't want war. We want a reunification. In our national hymn there is a verse that calls for our brothers over there to be with us again. And we want to help them be freer. But in their national hymn, they just sing to their "Genossen" [comrades], never to us.—Sven

These are the words of twelve-year-old Sven, who lives with his parents and eight-year-old sister in southern West Berlin, in the district of Steglitz. I shall refer to those words at various points throughout this section. In this statement, as was the case in all of our discussions, Sven demonstrates a remarkably perceptive intelligence along with a complicated array of feelings in regard to East Berlin and his (and his nation's) relationship to it. That is often the central concern of these children: just what is to be the nature of their relationship to East Berlin and the German Democratic Republic? In addressing that question they inevitably try to establish what it is that the nations on either side of the Wall stand for. The frequently posed question "Why does the Wall exist?" has no simple answer. Rather, it leads to other questions for which many children struggle to find reasonable answers.

Sven's statement touches on a large number of concerns: the reason for the division of Germany and the construction of the Berlin Wall, which dominates his drawing, figure 1; the geographic situation of Berlin—three hours from its corresponding nation and surrounded by the GDR; material differences between the two nations and pride in belonging to the richer of the two; a recognition that the expression of personal freedom varies considerably in East and West; awareness of the Soviet Union's significant involvement in GDR affairs; the manner in which East Germany attempts to foster in its children a deep antagonism toward the West; and a feeling on Sven's part of connection with and responsibility toward his East German neighbors, along with a distinct feeling of sadness in the face of the East's apparent rejection of his and his nation's efforts at reconciliation. Many of Sven's observations and sentiments resemble those of his peers, although there is a distinctive poignancy to his strong hopes for reunification that is not so clearly expressed by other children.

The year that I conducted this research happened to be the twentieth anniversary of the building of the Wall. School officials had pledged themselves to devote more classroom time to discussing with children the roots and political implications of the Wall. Yet because of the relative lack of firm guidelines in the teaching of history and civics in West Berlin's elementary schools, much of what children learned depended on the personal and political inclinations of specific teachers. Like Sven, most children in this city are somewhat unclear as to the precise origin of the Berlin Wall. In fact, in a questionnaire administered to a cross section of the West German population, including West Berlin, in 1981, only 52 percent of the participants responded correctly to the question: "Twenty years ago, on the 13th of August, 1961, something important happened in Germany. Do you happen to know what that was?" Of young people between the ages of sixteen and twenty-nine, only 44 percent knew that it was the start of construction of the Wall.[1] Nonetheless, West Berlin children frequently managed to get to the heart of the matter. When questioned as to the reason for the Wall's existence, they referred often to the Second World War, as well as to the differences between East and West that might require the Wall.

"We learn nothing about the Wall in school. We learn mostly from our parents, or television. I think it had something to do with the war. Hitler wanted to run the world; he wanted to conquer everyone else. But he lost. And then the other countries were so angry, they divided Germany. I can understand that. Fifty-five million people died in the war, and we started it." That statement of a twelve-year-old girl was echoed by a large number of children in West Berlin. It not only reveals an awareness of the relationship between a nation's past and present; it also suggests that the Wall is retribution for a nation's past transgressions, and as such it elicits complicated feelings in these youngsters. Many express a sad sense of complicity in those earlier crimes; one sixth grade teacher spoke of how she constantly has to remind her students that they are not responsible for the past. Others feel angry that they still must pay for the sins of their forebears. Yet whether they feel implicated in their nation's past or strive to distance themselves from it, that past is nonetheless ever present in the form of the Berlin Wall—a constant reminder and reproach.

Twelve-year-old Matthias put it this way:

> I think I was five or six the first time I saw the Wall. My father told me there was something I should see. He took me to the Wall where it runs along the other side of Wedding. At first I just couldn't understand it, even though my father was telling me why it was built. I just kept asking him *why*. It scared me; and I remember how sad I felt, too. And I thought then, and think now: "There must always be war." I was so sad. Today when I see the Wall, I always have the same thought: that pig Hitler. He started the war; he brought us to this. And it stinks! People are always saying we Germans are rotten, even though people my age, and even my father, didn't have anything to do with the war.

He has described a powerful lesson passed on from father to son; and his words are reinforced by those of a classmate of his, Constanza:

> Berlin is like a mini-Germany. Germany was divided after the war; and Berlin is divided too. Once it was the capital of Germany, and then Hitler came to power and began to kill the Jews, and tried to take over other countries. What he did was wrong, and he finally lost the war, and Germany was divided. I think they did that to punish us, but I'm not really sure. But whenever I see the Wall, I think of what Hitler did, and I

feel bad. And sometimes I think of how other people in other countries treat us, because we are German.

In the summer we go to Spain; we have a small house we rent there. When we go, we usually drive, and have to go through France on our way. Well, last year we stopped in some small town in France, and my mother got very upset because she heard someone say "German pigs," or something like that. We don't hear it a lot, but it made me think about why people might hate us. And then *I* got upset, too. I didn't start the war; and my mother was only a girl then. But I still end up feeling bad; it's my country that did those things, even if I didn't. Sometimes I even wish I wasn't German; then people wouldn't hate me.

The task of these two children, and many like them, is to somehow come to terms with a painful and complicated national past without at the same time losing too much self-esteem. In response to their daily confrontation with that past (their experience in a divided city, or the spiteful words of still bitter Europeans), many children seem to turn on their nation and on themselves to varying degrees.

"I hate Germans," said twelve-year-old Helmut. "I hear about what we did to the Jews and all I want to do is go somewhere else to live. I don't know how we could have done it; we're not good people. I will leave Berlin as soon as I can. I don't know where I will go, just somewhere where there is a job for me." Such a statement is sad and chilling, but not all that unusual. Here is Matthias once more:

I don't like Germans, even though I, too, am a German. When I think of what they are like, I can only think of bad things: brutality, a difficult language, simpleminded, exaggerated, and lots of terrorism. I can't imagine spending my whole life here; and when I am old enough I will move to Australia. Because I hate Germany, yes. And also because here we are in the middle of the United States and Russia, and if there is a war, we will be the first to be killed. At least in Australia I will have a better chance to live.

The intensity of Matthias's reproach toward his nation and himself is more extreme than that of many of his peers and suggests underlying difficulties with self-esteem that are not simply dependent on the historical and political issues of which he speaks. But the psychological and the political do get linked up in his mind, and in the minds of many other young people; history and politics are elements of their personal psychology. And the

Wall is that unavoidable reminder of a period in a nation's life that might be more easily forgotten elsewhere.

Several studies conducted throughout West Germany suggest that fewer and fewer Germans are willing to express pride in their nation. To the question "Are you proud to be German?," posed in 1981, only 35 percent of those questioned answered "definitely." Of those under thirty, only 20 percent answered likewise. Of those under thirty who said they were definitely proud to be German, only 26 percent would consider leaving their country to live elsewhere, while of those who did not feel proud of their nationality, 49 percent would gladly leave their country.[2] Clearly these West Berlin children are not alone in their very mixed allegiance to their homeland.

Yet I spoke with several children who, though well aware of the particularly shameful aspects of German history, maintained a more defensive posture in the face of the Wall and its antecedents, as well as adverse reactions voiced by outsiders. Twelve-year-old Michael expressed his views this way: "I know if it wasn't for Hitler, Germany would probably still be one nation today. I know he started the war and that he killed a lot of Jews. That is terrible. But he also did good things for the country; there wasn't so much 'Kaos' then like there is now, and not so many demonstrations. And people had jobs, too." This last issue is very important to Michael, as his father is out of work and has been for several months. He continues:

> Sometimes I get really sick to my stomach when we drive by the Wall. I don't usually see it, because we live near Tegel; it's easy to forget it's there. I think I am used to it; but sometimes I wonder if I'll ever get used to it. Why is it there? I'm not even sure who built it; but I think they did "over there." But I'm not sure why they did. I just know if it wasn't for Hitler, there would probably be no Wall. And when tourists see the Wall, they probably think of Hitler and of how bad Germany was. But Hitler wasn't just bad; and we're not just bad either. I just try to remember the good things; this is my country, and I know it's not just the way tourists see it.

For most of these children it is simply impossible to ignore the past. It faces them squarely every time they want to drive out of the city or take a walk in the outlying countryside: the Berlin Wall. How they come to terms with that past varies from child to child. Yet most of these children acknowledge, often quite hauntingly, that it does matter a good deal to them what sort of a country they belong to and, consequently, what sort of people *they* are.

And it is that kind of inquiry—who am I? What do I stand for?—that requires children to look carefully not only to the past, but to the present as well. Given the dramatic political circumstances that inform their lives, they cannot help but look around, ask questions pertaining to their situation, and arrive at some conclusions. Naturally their attention is frequently drawn to the Wall, because of the ways in which it restricts their lives and, perhaps more importantly, because of the way it hides from view the city of East Berlin and that world of state socialism.

For many West Berlin children, East Berlin remains an enigma; the sheer face of the Wall draws their vision toward the East yet denies satisfaction, veiling that which it highlights. The impression that most children have of East Berlin and the GDR consists of various facts acquired in school or through the media, personal observations made during border crossings and the subsequent car or train rides through East German countryside, or in moments spent peering from one of the numerous viewing platforms adjacent to the Wall. Some draw upon family stories told in the home or, for those children with relatives in the East, personal experience of life "over there." All children rely, too, on a liberal dose of imagination. Thus East Berlin is not only the object of fairly realistic appraisals made by West Berlin's children; like the Wall itself, it serves as a blank screen of sorts, on which children can project particular wishes and fears of a political, psychological, and moral nature.

Who are these people who live their lives hidden from view by the Wall? Following are two statements made by a pair of West Berlin boys, each twelve years old. They use remarkably different terms in defining their particular relationship with their neighbors to the east, and in so doing they reflect the two most frequently heard views held by the West Berlin children with whom I spoke.

West Berlin belongs to the FRG, and East Berlin belongs to Russia. But the people over there are like us. We were all Germans once—same religion, same ideas, same language. The Russians built the Wall because doctors were all coming over to the West where they could make more money and travel wherever they want. Over there people are trapped; I feel sorry for them.—Boris

For me, Germany is the Federal Republic. The East is *no* Germany— absolutely no country as far as I'm concerned. Maybe an in-between country. I cannot understand the people over there. I understand the language but not the meaning. They are foreigners to me, just like the Turks here in Berlin. If the Wall were gone, then I would understand them.—Carsten

Like Sven, whose words opened this discussion, Boris recognizes a certain kinship with the residents of the GDR, based not only on immediate family ties but on certain qualities that might be considered more "abstract": religion, ideas, language. He indicates that it is these very qualities that bring a people together and that any division of those people, at least in the case of Germany, can only be instigated from without (by the Russians). Boris sees the people of East Germany as "trapped" by the Russians, against their will; as such, they are deserving of his sympathy and concern. It is this ability to trace the connections between these two nations that allows Boris, and other children like him, to locate some sense of shared nationality beneath the confines of ideology. Often this ability is enhanced when a child has relatives "over there," such as eleven-year-old Ilke: "Why do they [the Allies] have to occupy us, like the Russians do the GDR? We should be rejoined with the people over there. It's not fair. We all have relatives over there; and we should be able to live together. We are all Germans."

Of course, this is the message many of these children receive not only from their parents and their own experience of visiting or being visited by grandparents from the East, but from their teachers. They are reminded often of their relation to and responsibility for their "fellow" Germans in the East. Since the war's end, and the subsequent division of Germany, the guiding vision of West German political life and Ostpolitik has been the hope of reunification. The most important holiday in West Berlin has been the "Tag der deutschen Einheit," the Day of German Unity, which commemorates the workers' uprising in East Berlin on June 17, 1953. On that day workers all over the GDR put down their tools to demonstrate against excessively high production quotas; and the Soviet Union retaliated violently. Although most children are not at all sure about the significance of the day, they welcome it as a school holiday. However, children who do have close ties with relatives in the East and those who in some other manner manage to feel a strong connection to the "other" German state often speak of reunification as the bringing together of a family that has been forcefully divided. Sven's statement expresses quite poignantly that desire, along with his confusion and sadness over the apparent East German "refusal" to consider rejoining the West.

Two interesting questionnaires administered by the Allensbach Institute addressed the issue of reunification with a range of West Germans, including those living in West Berlin. To the question "Do you hope very much for a reunification, or is that not very important to you?," 62 percent of the overall 1981 sample said yes. Of those between sixteen and twenty-nine, only 44 percent responded in kind. Of those questioned who have relatives in the East, 74 percent answered yes, while only 54 percent of those without relatives "over there" did likewise. When asked "Do you believe that East and West Germany will rejoin one another, or not?," approximately 65 percent answered in the negative, and only 13 percent responded positively.[3]

As hopes for reunification become weaker, there is talk of replacing the "Tag der deutschen Einheit" with the "Tag der Verfassung," Constitution Day. Until recently that day has been virtually ignored, for to honor the West German constitution would be to acknowledge the unlikely prospect of reunification. I cannot help but wonder how the children of West Berlin will feel about the East when they no longer have relatives over there, and when their government begins to accept more firmly the continuing existence of two separate German states. Quite possibly they will come to view East Germany as they do other German-speaking nations such as Austria and Switzerland.

Whether a child sees the East as related or alien will have much to do with how he looks at other aspects of the East and compares his world to that "other" world. For some children it is not only politically but psychologically convenient to perceive the East as alien, and hence as an object of fear toward which hostility and distrust are directed. Such may be the case with children like Carsten, a boy who has never been to East Berlin, yet has traveled westward through the GDR on his way to West Germany. For him the GDR is indeed an in-between country, a place to be passed through on his way elsewhere. More importantly, he demonstrates a rather subtle appreciation of the differences between the two countries that may outweigh the fact that they have a common language and cultural past. After more than thirty years of consolidating their power and authority, the FRG and the GDR are worlds apart ideologically, economically, and socially. When Carsten says he cannot understand the people over there "because of the Wall," he perceptively acknowledges the two very different realities the Wall separates. And although he may have his more deeply personal reasons for insisting on the radical differences between these two nations, he is also picking up and giving voice to certain political realities.

Many children share his views, although when pressed, several of them could not specify what it was that created such an unbridgeable gap between these two neighboring systems. For many, no doubt, the Wall itself was reason enough to assume there were drastic differences between East and West. Its presence is indeed the most visible indication of those differences. "Yes we do speak the same language in both countries, but we're different because of the border." This was a view I heard quite often, though more often than not children grounded those differences between two groups of people in the conditions of their respective national experience. "Even though they speak German, they're different. You see, over there they can't travel like we can. And they built the Wall because they were afraid the people would visit West Berlin and then decide to stay here." Children not only are aware that people with much in common can nonetheless differ significantly depending on the circumstances of their lives, but many recognize a distinction to be made between a government and the people it presumably governs.

A survey conducted in 1979, once again by the Allensbach Institute, explored further the feelings of West Germans toward their East German neighbors. The question was: "Imagine you are on vacation on the Black Sea. One day you meet another German there. During conversation you discover that he comes from the GDR, and lives there. What do you think in that moment when you find this out?" A list of possible answers was provided, none of them mutually exclusive. To the statement "I would be curious to talk with him," 71 percent of the entire sample agreed, and 80 percent of those between sixteen and twenty-nine did. But to the possible response "I think as Germans we would understand one another quite well on foreign territory," only 50 percent of both groups agreed, which is significantly less than the number who agreed in 1970.[4] Differences do exist and are perceived by a large number of West Germans. Of course, a questionnaire cannot get behind such responses, but these are nevertheless revealing about certain trends in attitudes.

Sometimes this strong sense of a basic difference turns into cause for casting aspersions on the East. What is not entirely understood is, at times, hated. "We call them 'Ostschweine' (east pigs) over there. Sometimes we go to the observation platforms along the Wall and shout at them." Yet not all of this hostility is projection elicited by mystery. Some children have direct experience with life in the GDR, primarily through relatives living

Figure 1

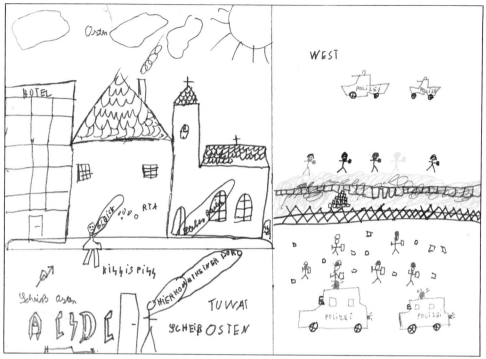

Figure 2

Figure 3

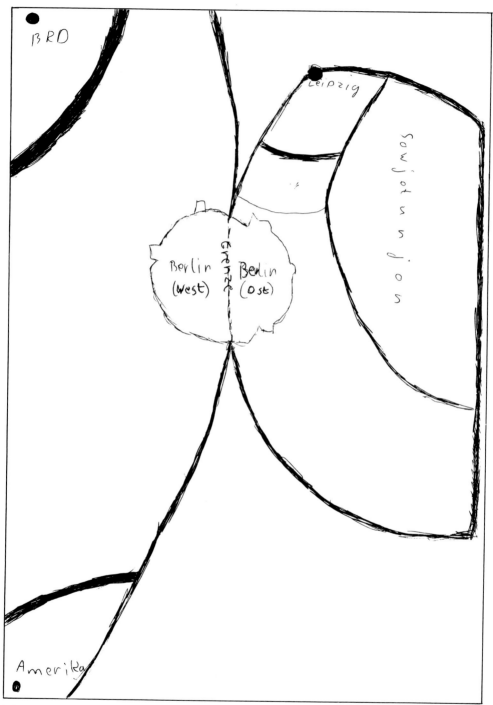

Figure 4

Figure 5

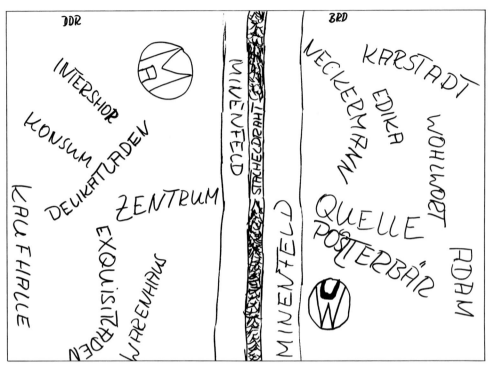

Figure 6

Figure 7

Figure 8

there. Others have direct experience of the particular horror of the Wall, as they live in direct proximity to it. Following is a brief account by twelve-year-old Brigitte, who lives in the working class district of Kreuzberg in direct sight of the Wall. The facts of her story were reported in newspaper accounts, as are all such events.

> I can see the Wall from my living room window. Yes, I forget about it sometimes, because it's always there. I was born here, and always remember the Wall being there. When I was little we used to play "border patrol" down there, but now I don't spend much time near it. Sometimes we hear their jeeps going by in "no-man's-land," and at night their alarms go off if someone tries to escape, or maybe they just have practice in case someone tries to escape.
>
> Well, two weeks ago someone did try. It was at night, and it's usually pretty quiet here—when all of a sudden I heard a lot of guns being fired over there. I knew someone was trying to get over, and I started to pray that he would make it. But I knew he wouldn't, and I felt so bad for him. A lot of people heard it too, and they got up and went to the Wall and started shouting and cursing at them over there. My mother let me go out with her and I shouted too. Then we started bringing garbage and other stuff over to the Wall and we set it on fire and let the wind blow the stinking smoke over to them. Everyone was so angry and some people were crying. I still wonder who it was that night; his family must be so sad. It's not fair, how they can't leave if they want to. And now I just hate the GDR, for what they do to the people.

This was an extremely powerful experience for Brigitte, and one that is not shared by many of her peers. Yet many children have an experience or two that, in similar ways, crystallize their attitudes toward the East. These experiences may fuel their anger and lead to a complete rejection of the system *and* people "over there."

These feelings frequently are conveyed through jokes. Kids say that the abbreviation for the Deutsche Demokratische Republik, DDR, stands for "drei doofe Russen" (three stupid Russians) or "*d*eutsche *D*achelrennbahn" (German dachsund raceway). The joke going around during my visit referred to Erich Honecker, president of the GDR, returning to East Berlin from a trip abroad. He is surprised, as no one comes to greet him at the airport. In the city he is further taken aback, as there are no crowds cheering him along Karl Marx Allee. Thoroughly perplexed, he heads toward his office; on his way he notices a small hole in the Wall. On arriving at his office he finds a note on his desk: "You're the last one out, Erich. Be sure to turn out the lights." There is not always much laughter at this joke, but children will tell it over and over. The joke also gets told by East Berlin children, and there it is freighted with a different significance. Although various negative experiences with the GDR may cause children to totally reject that nation and its people, they may, as in Brigitte's case, force them to distinguish between government and people like themselves and encourage a more ambivalent response toward East Germany.

In spite of the apparent dichotomy I have set up between those children who readily acknowledge their ties to the East and those who insist on the differences, most children manage to subscribe to both views without feeling troubled by the apparent contradiction. And as further discussion will demonstrate, this tolerance for ambiguity is not simply a reflection of an affinity for the people of the GDR versus hostility toward the system governing them. Many children also hold ambivalent views toward the system itself, sensing the advantages as well as the obvious disadvantages.

Before pursuing this line of inquiry—how children compare the world they live in with that on the other side of the Wall—I would like to address an issue of enormous consequence for children in West Berlin, and for their elders: the very visible presence of foreign guest workers in that city. How children contend with this is connected with their views of East Berlin and the GDR. When Carsten says that East Germans are "foreigners . . . just like the Turks," he puts a tremendous distance between himself and those East Germans. Most of the children with whom I spoke both fear and distrust the foreign nationals in their city, especially the Turks. Unlike Carsten, they generally make a significant distinction between Turks and East Germans. In fact, it appears that certain hostilities toward the East are tempered somewhat as the fear and aggressive feelings of these youngsters focus on the Turks in West Berlin. With these dark-haired, peculiarly garbed, strange-tongued foreigners present in their day-to-day lives, children do not perceive East Germans as so different, or so "bad."

"I don't mind the Italians or the Yugoslavs. But I hate the Turks. I can't understand them. They're not like us and don't belong here." This was something I heard frequently, especially among children living in the working class districts of Wedding, Kreuzberg, or Schöneberg, which by virtue of lower rents attract a large portion of foreign guest workers. Such districts are quite densely populated, with large numbers of old, expansive apartment houses that sometimes enclose up to three "Hinterhöfe," or inside courtyards. Such cramped living quarters were a product of the Industrial Revolution and were designed to house many workers as cheaply as possible. Little attention was therefore paid to lighting or ventilation, and even today these particular apartments overlooking dark and musty courtyards (which in winter fill with smoke from thousands of coal-burning stoves) are dank and depressing. For these working class children the "Ausländerproblem" is serious, whereas it is less so for their more well-off peers living in the comfort and seclusion of the wealthier districts to the west of the city: Dahlem, Charlottenburg, Tegel.

One twelve-year-old boy says it quite clearly. "There's a lot I love about Berlin: the parks, the lakes; you can play soccer everywhere. But I don't want to stay here; there are too many foreigners here. I know some of them are good, but some are terrible. And there just seem to be more here all the time. On my street I see more Turks than Germans now." Reasons for leaving Berlin include the foreign guest workers as often as they do the "island status" of the city.

But it is not simply the dramatic difference in culture that frightens children and leads them to vent their various hostilities on a particularly vulnerable group of people. Many of these children have fathers and/or mothers who are currently unemployed, and children (along with a good many adults) mistakenly blame the presence of Turkish guest workers for the rise in unemployment among Germans, and among their parents in particular. "These foreigners are taking our jobs. Look at all our unemployment here—and it's because of them! Pretty soon this will be a Turkish city if we don't do something. When I walk home from school, I see a Turk, a German, a German, then a Turk, a Turk, and another Turk. They're all over, and then they're even rude to us Germans. They act like kings here." Of course, much of what this eleven-year-old girl says is not true; studies indicate that the two groups, Germans and foreign guest workers, are not in competition for jobs.[5] But we are talking about children's perceptions, which are as much a reflection of their needs and longings as of reality. It is important to remember that many of these young people are themselves vulnerable—from hard-pressed, working families in a city that is visited and remembered for its glitzy, decadent cabaret world that is really only a small part of its day-to-day life.

Certainly economic insecurity can generate and play off of psychological insecurities, and both may lead to the harsh antagonism so often expressed by children toward the Turks in West Berlin. Occasionally such antipathy toward this particular group of foreign guest workers ends up muting a certain antagonism toward East Germany. Dissimilarities between East and West Germans are played down in relation to those between Turks and West Germans. As Freud reminded us, it is possible to bring a large number of people together in love, as long as there are others toward whom they can direct their aggressiveness.

I mention children's views toward "Gastarbeiter" in West Berlin not because those feelings overshadow their feelings toward East Berlin but because they are part of the rich texture of the political and moral lives of these children. The tide of feelings toward guest workers and the fact that West Berlin has become a haven of sorts for them have a definite influence on the views these children hold for their own nation. Like that child who loves much about Berlin but is angered by the presence (overwhelming and threatening to him) of so many foreigners, many young people feel a certain sense of betrayal by their city and by the powers that be. Those presumably in charge appear to be doing nothing to alleviate these particular fears of children and their families alike, nor have they successfully addressed the very critical economic concerns of these same individuals. Obviously, children in West Berlin draw on internal affairs along with a comparative view of East and West in coming to their various political and moral convictions. In some respects the East appears more attractive insofar as it is less subject to the particular ills of the West that these children confront.

Whether looking at their own society or at that of their neighbors across the Berlin Wall, the children I talked to repeatedly raised specific issues of concern to them. And their regard for either West or East Berlin is in good part predicated on the manner in which those cities address these concerns. Some of these are clearly apparent in several of the foregoing statements: the quality of material comforts; the degree to which certain personal freedoms can be exercised, as well as the degree to which sufficient controls and protection are provided. In addition, many children were concerned with the manner in which a sense of fair play and justice is exercised in both cities. These comparisons draw not only upon an awareness of the "facts," but also upon recognition of the "ideal" on which each society sets its sights.

All children spoke of the economic disparities between East and West, and they indicated that they were well aware of the general absence of luxury items as well as certain essentials in East Berlin and elsewhere in the GDR. On the surface this *is* the most striking difference between the two systems; and when children visit relatives "over there" or drive through the East German countryside on the way to West Germany, they come face to face with the obvious discrepancies in automobiles or housing. When they describe this variance in material well-being, children often make rather peculiar observations that suggest not only a recognition of a genuine disparity, but a need to effectively "put down" the GDR in this fashion.

> It's dirtier over there. I saw the post office there once, when I visited my Oma. It was much dirtier than ours.—Eleven-year-old girl

> The clothes over there are not as pretty as ours. And the food is awful; the ice cream is gummy or something, not good; and the bread and cake taste, well, they taste strange somehow.—Twelve-year-old girl

> Over there is not as good as here. There they live bad, with never enough to eat or drink. They're always staring at us when we come to visit. We have a BMW, and they have their Trabis [Trabant, the most popular and affordable of East German cars]. . . . Since they built the Wall, we have all the good things here—food and other things—and they don't.—Eleven-year-old boy

Although children from diverse socioeconomic backgrounds made similar references to the material discrepancies between East and West, those differences take on a special significance for many of the working class children of Wedding or Kreuzberg. Like the eleven-year-old girl mentioned earlier who remarked, "Sometimes I think there are two West Berlins . . . the rich Berlin that everyone wants to see, and then us," most of these children are all too aware of the economic disparities that lie at the heart of their own city, and they know that they are not at the receiving end of a large number of the benefits that go to their peers in Dahlem or Tegel. For many of these children the close proximity of a "poor" nation such as the GDR (a German nation at that) allows them to assert themselves over their socialist neighbors at least. Many of these children who resent their comparative poverty in the face of the often garish displays of wealth in West Berlin speak with a distinct measure of pride of their "wealth" in contrast to the poverty of East Berlin: there is someone to look down on, just as they are looked down on, or, worse yet, ignored. What this means for many children is that they are able, by virtue of their geopolitical situation, to turn a potentially critical eye away from certain glaring inequities in their own system and to look instead to the East, and be grateful to have more than "they" do.

Twelve-year-old Tanya made this quite clear to me during one of our walks through Grunewald, the large, quite beautiful forest—dotted with lakes and grassy fields—that lies to the west of the city. During warm weather we would occasionally make the forty-minute trip, by bus and subway, from her home in Wedding to the expanse of Grunewald. Like most Berliners, Tanya greatly appreciates the relative quiet and open spaces afforded by the various city parks. They are a much-needed respite from the harsh, noisy, and crowded life she knows in Wedding, where she shares a three-room apartment with her mother and older sister and her sister's two young children.

On this May day we were making our way through the wealthy neighborhoods adjoining Grunewald, passing by enormous villas that had been built at an earlier more peaceful time in the city's history. It was in reference to these that she spoke. "I'd sure like to live in this area. It seems so far away from Wedding. Sometimes it seems like another city that has nothing to do with my life; and I'll go home and hate my apartment. It's so noisy and crowded! But then when I visit my aunt "over there," I realize it's not so bad for me here. We have a nice car, a good television . . . a lot more than they do in the East."

Although most children did not make that connection as explicitly as Tanya, they know what she is talking about. In fact, several go one step further: they not only recognize the comparative austerity of the East but occasionally perceive the proximity of that world, and the fact that it surrounds West Berlin, as a potential threat to their way of life. And of course the East *is* a potential threat—the threat to take away individual possessions as well as a particular way of ordering experience. As one young boy said, "The Wall was built because we were afraid they'd all come over and get jobs here and take our money back with them. Then they'd be rich and we'd be poor."

All of these comments pertaining to the economic disparity between two systems were delivered in the context of larger statements. By presenting them in isolation, one runs the risk of overestimating the importance of material well-being for many of these youngsters. Certainly it is important; they live in a world that is constantly stressing just that. But it is misleading to say that this is all that matters to children as they try to evaluate two very different yet related political systems. In fact, these comparisons along material lines sometimes give children pause to call into question their own values and those of a nation that does not always appear willing to address its own built-in injustices and economic inequities. Once again, the East (in this case, the ideals it proclaims) serves as a point of comparison with the West.

> Here in Berlin there are just too many shops. Wherever you look— shops. And expensive ones. And there are a lot of people here who can't go into these shops because they're poor. And then there are the Punkers who think they own the world; and the Poppers ["slick," well-heeled young people] who get all dressed up and drink wine and champagne somewhere while some people here can only manage to get a loaf of bread every day. It's just not fair here. I know it's more free here than "over there," but it's not all *good*. I think in the East they want more people to have the same amount of money, so maybe there won't be really rich people and really poor people like here.

These are the words of twelve-year-old Alex, a girl who is not unique among my "informants" in her concern for those less well off than herself and in her recognition that those inequities of which she speaks have something to do with a particular economic and political system of which she is a member (and, on occasion, a critical one at that). Money, its importance, the unequal distribution of it, is very much on the minds of these children. I am not saying that such is not the case elsewhere, but children living in West Berlin have another quite different and nearby point of reference that occasionally fuels their nascent economic and moral critiques of the West.

Young Helmut once started a conversation with the following exclamation: "Without money no one could make it in this world!" And he went on to explain what had led him to this outburst. His family had been trying for the past six months to find another apartment, no easy task in West Berlin. Those apartments that were affordable were too small, while those that could comfortably accommodate his family were beyond the means of his working mother—a secretary at a local police station. Helmut's mother was feeling the financial squeeze, and her son was suffering under and resenting the growing family tension as the search went on. Money would, or so it seemed to him, alleviate many of his worries. Helmut then presented his view of the economic stratification of his society, along with his judgment thereof.

> There are the rich people—the actors, soccer players, bankers, and businessmen, people who inherit money. Then there are the middle level people like us, who can afford certain things, but not everything; and

then there are the poor, who can't afford anything. Although we're in the middle, it still never feels like enough. I notice prices keep going up, and my mother is having trouble shopping. And we can't afford a decent apartment. . . .

I don't think it's fair that salaries are so different. If I were in charge, I'd set one salary—maybe every family would get DM 2,500 each month, at *least*. It's not right that some people have so much they don't know what to do with their money, or what else to buy. . . . I'm not saying I'd want to live "over there," but at least there are not real rich people like there are here. People earn pretty much the same, and that seems fairer.

Neither Helmut nor Alex has any way of evaluating the discrepancies between theory and practice that exist as surely in East Germany as they do elsewhere. But they are responding as much to an ideal as to an observable reality. East Germany may be poor, it may be dirty, it may circumscribe individual freedoms, and toward all that these children extend their disapproval. Yet in their eyes East Germany has also tried to address certain economic and moral issues that are particularly relevant to them.

Perhaps the most moving statement in this regard was made by Matthias, for whom the streets of West Berlin provide all he needs for drawing up his own moral inventory. One such street is the Kurfürstendamm, commonly known as Ku'damm. On special occasions—his birthday or graduation from "Grundschule"—we would take the half-hour trip, by bus and subway, from his home in Wedding to this long, glittery, café-studded boulevard in the heart of West Berlin—a tourist mecca lined with expensive boutiques, restaurants, and sex shops, at the end of which looms the Gedächtniskirche (Kaiser Wilhelm Memorial Church), a bombed-out reminder of an earlier time. Here we would dine at Burger King and then stroll past the numerous street artists, perhaps see a movie. Matthias was somewhat in awe of it all; Ku'damm is at a far remove from his home in Wedding. Yet he kept his head about him, and one such outing became the occasion for the following words.

You really need money here on Ku'damm. When I walk down this street, I just think of how I could spend my money if I had a lot, and sometimes I just think I have to spend it any way I can—that it doesn't matter how. I don't think I want much, but when I am here I begin to forget that. I see a motorcycle, a car, even a necklace, and I want them, and I begin to dream of them. And that's no good. People here always want to have, have, have. Here it seems like the main thing in life is money and good things. But that's not how it should be. The most important thing is contact with others; and people who are greedy have no contact. People end up hating each other because of money.

Over there in East Berlin they have socialism. I don't think it's good that they can't travel where they want; but I hear that there aren't any real rich people there, that everyone is more equal. I think that's more fair. Sometimes I think the Wall keeps *that* away from us, too—not just the Russians. And it would be better if we had some of that, too. Sometimes I think we should have poverty every six years, and then pick up again. To learn not to want everything, to learn to think about what we really need and don't need. I think after a couple of poverty catastrophes we'd be okay.

Insofar as East Germany addresses these particular issues of fairness more satisfactorily than West Germany, it fares better in the estimation of these children than the West. Yet, once again, this is balanced against other qualities of life and ideology in the East, many of which children do not find so congenial.

Those other qualities have to do with the way in which a system establishes a balance between expression of individual freedoms and control. As I have suggested, this is a terribly important concern for many children not only because it is in this respect that the FRG and the GDR differ so significantly, but because it reflects what children go through on a psychological and a familial level—their struggle between "freedom" and "responsibility."

Although it is convenient, when speaking of the differences between state socialism as it exists in the GDR and western capitalism as it appears in the FRG, to declare that the West allows for more individual freedom while the East is repressive (which is in good part true), it would be wrong to assume that the differences can be so simply stated, or that those differences inevitably point to the "superiority" of West over East. It would be equally wrong to assume that children are only able to perceive and articulate that black-and-white dichotomy. Many of them, in fact, seek actively for the various exceptions to the rule and often look beneath supposed "advantages" of each system to their flip side, their occasional disadvantages.

The views these children hold toward the East are, of course, inextricably bound up with their experience in West Berlin. If things were perfect in the West, it would be quite easy for children to point smugly to the deficiencies of the East. Yet, because such is not the case, and because children *know* this and are well aware of the shortcomings of their own city's life, they not only suspect that there are positive as well as negative aspects to life on the other side of the Wall, but many of them wishfully believe that perhaps there exists in the East that which is lacking in the West—either in their family situation or in the larger life of their city. (See the case study of Klaus at the end of this chapter.)

Generally children are quick to point out the glaring injustices of life in the East, and it is only later that they will allow themselves more careful consideration of the situation and express some of their ambivalent responses. Once again, Sven's words are reminiscent of the feelings expressed by many of these children: "They're less free over there than we are. They can't say what they like. If someone goes to Alex Platz and shouts 'I hate the GDR,' the Russians will grab him right away, and throw him in jail. Here, if you shout you don't like the mayor, nobody bothers you. You can say what you like." Children's knowledge of the repression that is a part of East German life comes to them in a variety of ways—from classroom instruction or parents' stories, or from dramatic experience such as Brigitte underwent alongside the Wall.

The two sorts of "freedom" that many of these children focus on are freedom of speech and freedom to travel, both of which are substantially limited in East Germany. Children appear quite responsive to the way freedom of speech gets handled—both as it is denied in East Germany and as it is occasionally overexercised in their own city. How either government addresses this issue is significant for many children, in part because they recognize in these efforts their own experience with an authority that is closer to home. The apparent abuse of authority in the East reminds children of their occasional, or perhaps frequent, "bad" experiences with parents. Their image of GDR authority acquires a prohibitive quality and may even come to resemble the strictly punitive aspects of the child's own conscience. That is a very potent image for many children, and though the Wall serves to protect them from it, they also perceive certain advantages to such a system.

In order to appreciate what those advantages might be, it is first necessary to discuss an element of life in West Berlin that figures quite significantly in the day-to-day lives of these children and contributes to their ambivalence toward freedom in general and freedom of expression in particular: the "Hausbesetzerszene," or "house squatters scene." Actually it is not entirely appropriate to speak of the "Hausbesetzerszene." Rather,

I am referring to the frequent street demonstrations that were often a part of that group's efforts at drawing attention to housing conditions in the city. In that the city attracts thousands of outsiders and malcontents, such "Demos" often turned into wild rampages and were often the means by which groups of various social and political persuasions voiced their plain hostilities as much as their ideas or slogans. They could be frightening displays of unrestrained aggression, not always easily subdued by police efforts. Twelve-year-old Nicole recalls one such demonstration:

> It was sometime last month, and my friend and I were coming home from the park, and we ran right into the middle of a Demo at Leopoldplatz. There were lots of Punkers there and they were really rude. They were spitting on the police and yelling and breaking windows. It was really "verrückt" [crazy]. And we got scared—but not just because of the Punkers. The police were also very rough, hitting people on the head with their sticks. We got away without getting hurt—but that's going on all over Berlin, all the time.

It is the arbitrariness of the violence that is so disturbing to children, the not knowing when a demonstration will materialize, or to what extent it will be violent and out of control. Although the presence of police can be reassuring at such times, Nicole's response to police behavior (one I heard from many children) suggests that their apparent loss of control is just as frightening, if not more so, than that of the demonstrators. At such moments chaos reigns, and nobody appears to be really in charge. In contrast, the East may appear somewhat more benign—a place that, at least, is safe from this kind of craziness. Twelve-year-old Alex had this to say: "Yes, it's more 'free' here than over there, but it's not all good. Freedom means that we have all these demonstrations here—people who just want to destroy, never fight *for* something. I think they shouldn't be allowed to demonstrate. If you tried to do that in East Berlin, you'd get shot. I don't think that's right, but it should be stricter here."

Perhaps it is fairest to say that although the East is too severe in its application of control, its presence serves as a reminder that it is possible to exert more control than exists in West Berlin. Many children draw lessons from both cities and arrive at their own conclusions as to how the issue of control versus freedom might best be addressed. In her drawing contrasting East and West (figure 2), twelve-year-old Claudia dramatizes the major conflicts she perceives in both cities. To the right, in West Berlin, a battle rages between police and demonstrators. Each group stares at the other over a burning barricade—a common sight in the city. To the left of her picture is East Berlin, wherein she draws a world in black ("Trauerfarbe," or mourning colors, she says). A house stands at the center, flanked by a church to the right and a hotel to the left. The scene is divided by the Wall, behind which a border guard is shouting, "Stand where you are!," as a man escapes over the Wall into the West. The Wall itself is covered with graffiti—reflecting cultural interests (the names of rock groups, the logo for the "Hausbesetzerszene") and political concerns ("shitty East"). Altogether, the picture effectively portrays the chaos of the West and the repression of the East. By virtue of its symmetry—the burning barricade in the West, the Wall in the East—this picture also suggests that the various polarities in Claudia's life are more complicated than just East versus West.

Still, there is, on the part of many children, a sense that life in the East is less hectic and less violent than in the West (an observation also made by older, more politically savvy travelers). They feel that certain needs that are often left unmet at home have a better chance of being fulfilled in the East. These "needs" range from the need to engage in meaningful activity, be it in the child's or the adult's life, to a somewhat vaguer, though no less important need for "Ruhe," peace and calm. Children consider each of these, depending on their personal circumstances.

Connie, twelve, voices the complaints of many children when she says, "Here kids can usually do what they want. There's nobody telling you what to do. But there's nothing to do, either—watch television is all usually. People don't help kids find things to do. And over there it's worse in the other way: kids are always told what to do, what to think. But sometimes I think they might not be so bored, and people at least pay attention to them." A society that abandons its young people and their intense need to feel useful as well as to have something to believe in and care about pays the price in the growing boredom and apathy of those children. Connie's words remind me somewhat of Alex's comment that it is important to use freedom to "fight *for* something." Somehow, the freedom many of these kids are given can be confusing, and it frequently leaves them feeling rudderless. They look to the adults around them, to their "society," and ask for direction, something to believe in, something worth doing, or fighting for. And many feel let down, set adrift in the screaming variety and consumerism that is West Berlin. The GDR again begins to appear more willing to address—even if too harshly—those concerns.

Matthias goes on to address other needs he and his peers feel:

To work and to be free, that is important. Over there, people have work. That is good. But they are not free. Here we are freer, but there is less work. People have to feel needed. There's so much unemployment now; and I read somewhere that 50 percent of suicides are people out of work. If I were mayor of Berlin, the first thing I'd do is get people jobs. Then I'd take care of housing problems, so that people who need apartments get them without having to use all their salary for rent. These are two things people "over there" get without having to fight. That's the best thing about life in East Berlin.

Freedom and security—two sides of the same coin, each handled quite differently in these neighboring cities. And how these are addressed by a society is a very important consideration children make in becoming members of (or losing faith in) a particular political system. Yet there are also more personal issues that are constantly brought up as children assess the relative merits of East and West, as the words and drawing (figure 3) of young Michael suggest: "I have been to East Berlin a few times to visit my relatives. They have a really nice garden, and that's what I remember most. Whenever we visit them, I think it must be nice over there in some ways. It's so quiet and pretty compared to where I live. And the kids are nice and it's easier to play there—less dangerous—because there is less traffic when you play. Sometimes I think it could be so easy there. . . ." In his drawing, Michael manages to portray the peaceful, homey feelings he has for the East—the garden is lush and protected by its own wall—while the West is composed of a series of block houses, which he drew in quickly and with no concern for detail.

Yet such feelings of attraction toward life in the East, albeit sincere, are often held in check by children's awareness of the varieties of repression there. The restriction most obvious from the outside is the prohibition on travel. This is significant for children because of the way its repression or expression (as with freedom of speech) links up with certain psychological issues, and because the "need" to travel is a recognizable German trait. Since the wanderings of Goethe, Germans have romanticized travel, and it is their inability to travel beyond East Bloc countries that frustrates East Germans and evokes empathetic responses from West Germans. Although they are forced to have different destinations, both national groups are recognized as the most widely traveled within their respective sides of Europe. To the question, "If you had more money or time, what would you most like to do?," posed to West Germans in 1979, 82 percent of all respondents under age twenty-five listed travel as their first choice.[6]

Of course most West Berliners end up restricting their travel to other ideologically compatible nations, and economics rather than a centralized bureaucracy helps determine those various destinations—generally Greece, Spain, or for the particularly hard-pressed, West Germany. Eastern Europe is avoided for a variety of reasons, from a general dislike for the political systems that prevail there and the controlled nature of the visitor's experience, which presumably precludes the possibility for relaxation, to the daily currency exchange quotas which would make such a trip of any duration unaffordable. The father of one of my young informants commented on this: "I've lived eighty kilometers from Poland all my life, and I am raising my children here as well. Yet we are more familiar with Spain, which is much farther away! I never even met a Pole until six years ago!"

On another level, the travel restrictions of the GDR make it virtually impossible for individuals under sixty-five to visit family in the West. And children in West Berlin are well aware of that, although their empathy for East Germans on this count is not simply a product of severed family ties but of an appreciation of the ability to leave a place when necessary, to wrestle with everydayness by a change of locale. (This last is especially true in West Berlin, where everyone speaks of "Mauerkrankheit.")

Of course, many of the children I knew were not particularly well off, and their freedom to travel was definitely limited by economic realities. Many working class families are lucky if they get out of West Berlin twice a year, to West Germany once and perhaps to Spain or Greece. Yet what appears to matter to these children is that in the West there are no rules, no government officials, preventing them from exercising their particular freedoms, although, to be sure, several of them have already begun to draw the connection between economic security and the ability to enjoy certain "guaranteed" freedoms.

Over there they can't travel where they want; they can only go to other countries like them—the CSSR or Poland—but never to the West or to America. I think they're afraid if they're allowed to leave, the people won't come back. But I think they would—that's their home. We come back to West Berlin whenever we go to Spain. But I really wish we could go to America. That's my dream—to see Disneyland. But my father says we won't be able to afford it for a few years, and maybe not even then. That really bothers me, because some kids *can* go, *now*. . . . Maybe we'll go someday . . . but they [in the East] will never be able to, even if they do save the money. That's too bad.—Twelve-year-old Annette

Annette's words once again reveal the use to which the presence of the GDR is put by so many young people. It allows children to divert certain dissatisfactions with their political system onto the East. They seem to feel, "Although there are problems and various inequities here, it could be worse, and *is* worse 'over there.' "

Annette also makes a rather striking observation in the middle of her statement when she refers to the fact that people "over there" consider the East their home and therefore must feel a certain loyalty that somehow transcends various political constraints. Children in West Berlin argued frequently and sometimes heatedly as to whether East Berlin residents were happy in the East or whether they would leave if they were given the chance. Many of these kids managed to articulate what Annette did: that "home" has to do with family and friends and a sense of place, and even if certain political restrictions were somewhat eased, people would certainly stay. However, many of these kids do not feel that family and friends are enough; they realize that "home" exists in a larger political context and as such is very much influenced by larger political issues. Such children indicate that the quality of the larger political environment contributes to how "at home" an individual will really feel. This whole essay, in fact, has been devoted to how children do or do not feel "at home" in their world.

That feeling of being "at home" is predicated on the feeling that the child is safe from danger, both internal and external. And for most of these children a central concern is to be protected from outside danger— invasion from the East or full-scale war. Many of these kids recognize that they are directly at the center of East-West tensions, as Manuela's drawing graphically indicates (see figure 4), and they fear the results of hostilities between those two nations. On the right side of her drawing looms the Soviet Union, while in the upper and lower left-hand corners of the page are America and the FRG. East and West Berlin are in the center, pulled in two directions by the superpowers. One twelve-year-old boy portrayed his fears in a stark drawing of East and West Berlin (figure 5). The two cities are here separated by a line (the Wall) etched in red. At the center of the picture is the Brandenburg Gate, which does indeed sit directly along the Wall, though it is also a symbol of a time when the city was not divided.

East Berlin is represented by a Russian tank with its gun aimed at the West, whereas West Berlin is represented by a park in this boy's neighborhood—a peaceful, pastoral scene threatened by the East. Some of these young people are hopeful that the worst will be averted, but many others have picked up on the national mood of fear and pessimism (focused as it was on the planned stationing of new American Pershing missiles on West German soil) that has encouraged the incorporation of such English phrases as "no future" in the German language.

The comments of children reflect this feeling of vulnerability. An eleven-year-old boy remarked, "We are in the middle between the U.S.A. and Russia. I have more fear of the Russians, though. America will help us. But what can we do if they want to fight? Sooner or later they will." The dependence on the United States is frequently expressed, as in these words of a twelve-year-old girl: "If America left, the Russians would move right in and we'd become part of the GDR. Well, maybe the French and British would help us, but the FRG couldn't help us by itself. It's not strong enough." Although comments like "I am more afraid of the Russians than the Americans," reveal the precarious nature of their situation, most young people see the United States presence as not only necessary but fortunate:

> The Amis are here, with the French and English, to protect us. I'm sure if the Amis left, there'd be another world war. Did you hear about the demonstration when your foreign minister came here? People were yelling "Amis raus" [Amis out]; but that's just crazy. I like the Americans; behind my house we can always see jeeps going by. I wave to them, and sometimes they wave back. They practice here, so they'll be ready in case there's a war. Over there they have so many tanks and jeeps and missiles. I'm afraid they and the Russians will fight us, so I'm really glad the Amis stay here.—Twelve-year-old girl

Although even the Americans acknowledge that their troops in West Berlin are primarily symbolic and unable to contain any genuine threat from the Soviets, the troops are a very visible and often reassuring presence for these children. This dependence, along with the fact that West Berlin is still technically "occupied" by the Allies and administered by them, sometimes leads children to say that West Germany is part of America, or "belongs" to America, just as the GDR belongs to the Soviet Union. Their allegiance is not simply to their nation but to that power which offers much-needed protection.

Yet because of the widespread opposition to the stationing of new

American missiles in West Germany, many of these children have acquired very mixed feelings toward their "protector" and are now beginning to feel caught in the middle, rather than unequivocally protected by the Amis. The mood among many children is now one of anxiety—their survival appears to be at stake.

> The Amis have maneuvers often; we see their tanks speeding by. They usually practice in Grunewald, but sometimes they're here behind the school in the park. You should see what they do to Grunewald, though! They really tear it up—just ruin it! But they need to practice for a real war. If they didn't, they couldn't beat the Russians. But I heard the other night that Reagan wants to destroy all of West Germany. He wants to try out the neutron bomb here. Someone said he wants to destroy Germany and make a new one. I'm afraid he just wants to destroy us. It's bad—I don't know who to trust.

Children in West Berlin have no doubt always worried about external threats coming from the East; how could they feel otherwise, given the clear presence of the Wall and the Soviet and East German soldiers on its other side? And it is likely that they have always acknowledged on some level the fact that they are smack in the middle of East and West, as well as surrounded geographically by a presumably hostile nation. In addition to all that, however, these children with whom I spoke also must contend with the fact that their own nation is unable to offer adequate protection, as well as the possibility that the nation that *would* protect them is also fallible and may indirectly be as much a threat to their existence as are the Soviets.

I am reminded of an incident that occurred when I was playing with two young boys in their schoolyard, and an American tank raced by along Afrikanerstrasse. Both boys immediately interrupted their play and ran toward the tank, waving and yelling in a fairly relaxed and friendly fashion. For some reason the tank stopped momentarily, at which point both boys were visibly seized with fear and panic, and ran back to the school. The protectors are also powerful and frightening in their military guise. This ambivalence was expressed by a teacher to his fifth grade class: "The Allies are here in Berlin, as they are the 'Schutzmächte' [defense powers], so to speak. . . . Or maybe it would be better to say 'Besatzungsmächte' [occupying powers], which is closer to the truth."

It is indeed a peculiar situation, one that contributes to the confusion many children feel about the status of their own nation, its relation to the United States and the GDR, and the dangerous position that Germany occupies. This uncertainty and ambivalence is once again rather poignantly stated by young Matthias:

> I know we're supposed to hate East Germany and Russia, and love the United States. Sometimes I do, but not always. It's not that simple. During the last war, Germany was beat by the Russians, *and* the French, English and Americans. Because of that, East Germany now belongs to Russia, and West Berlin belongs to America. I know I'm a German citizen, but America runs us here, you know. And I think the U.S. stays here because it gets good money by putting weapons over here. That's why I don't think the Amis will ever leave us. If they did, I think the Russians would move right in. They have so many tanks and soldiers over in East Germany. They're a lot stronger than we are here.
>
> But the Amis worry me, too. They're both doing the same thing: the Russians in East Germany, the Amis here. And I'm afraid if America stations neutron bombs here, there will be a war. And I don't think anyone will survive an atomic war. That's why I think war is worse than cancer. With cancer, maybe six million die. With war, we all die. I am very afraid of that.
>
> If that will happen, in Germany we will have to have a revolution, a civil war, to say "no" to America. We will all have to come out in the streets, and break windows, just like the "Hausbesetzer" do now.

What makes the situation of these children so compelling is that a particular political situation—West Berlin surrounded by the Wall and the GDR, a meeting place of socialism and capitalism, East and West—reflects and influences their psychological and moral as well as political concerns. For some, East Berlin is family, while others feel estranged from that city. Some want reunification; others want nothing to do with the GDR. For some the East possesses important moral attributes, while others see it as a place of severe restrictions of personal liberty, reinforced as they are by guns, dogs, and an imposing concrete wall. Yet regardless of their differences, all of these children inevitably *use* the facts of their political life, tether them to personal and psychological concerns, in order to come to some kind of moral and political understanding of their particular place in this world. Following is a brief case study of one young boy, Klaus. In it I hope to evoke those connections between a child's inner and outer world that help determine the ways in which he views his political and moral landscape.

Case Study: Klaus

I see Berlin as an island, since we're surrounded by the DDR. I worry a lot about what will happen if the Russians decide to attack the West. If that happens, we'll be lost; there are so many Russians on the other side of the Wall. My country, Germany, has close ties to America; we work together. So if Russia attacks America, they'll attack us also. We're stuck in between East and West here, and will suffer badly if there is a war. Yet I can't say I think there *will* be a war. Each side is afraid of the other, and both *must* know that a war between them means suicide for both. Still, I look at the Wall and see those guard towers and tanks, and I get worried. What will happen?

Twelve-year-old Klaus asks that last question with poignant urgency. He is a fairly lonely child, set apart from his peers by his intelligence, articulateness, and occasional "academic" attitude. Dubbed "Herr Professor" by his classmates, Klaus often feels isolated—not unlike the city he has just described. He lives in the working class district of Wedding with his grandmother, in a two-room apartment on the third floor of an old apartment house. The parlor windows overlook the street; from here Klaus can see the Bäckerei directly across the street, and if he peers to the right he can see the Aldi supermarket, small by American standards. It is primarily a residential street, with a few family-run shops. In the last few years this neighborhood has attracted increasing numbers of other "outsiders"— primarily Turkish guest workers. There are increasing reports of street crime in his area, and Klaus is as wary of the threats now facing him within his city as he is of those on the other side of the Wall. "I have nothing against them personally. They are here to do work we Germans don't want to do. But they're not like us, and I think soon there will be too many of them. Already on my street I see more Turks, it seems, than Germans. I used to feel safe here; now I'm not sure."

Klaus is not alone in his distrustful, if not antagonistic, regard of these "Gastarbeiter." Unlike his more well-to-do fellow citizens, he is forced to live in close proximity to his city's "guests"; for they, too, seek out those areas of West Berlin where rents are more affordable. Klaus is aware of the connection between class and certain attitudes, and occasionally he berates those people who, by virtue of the safety and comfort of their homes in the more exclusive residential districts of Dahlem or Lichterfelde, feel free to condemn the supposed intolerance of working class people like him and his family. "It's not that I don't like the Turks. And if I had my own house near

Grunewald, then I'd probably like them even more. But they are different from us; and there's more crime here than there used to be. Those rich people don't have to worry, the way we do." Perhaps so; yet Klaus's fears take on a greater magnitude at times, as he has recently lost the one place where he might have felt safe and protected: his home.

During the eight months preceding my meeting Klaus, his father had been in the hospital slowly dying from cancer. Klaus visited him rarely because, he says, his condition demanded as few "disturbances" as possible. When his father died, two months after I had met Klaus, he suffered a double loss. His mother had been in and out of hospitals herself for the past several years, due to a string of somatic and psychological complaints. The final illness of her husband was apparently more than she could bear, and her only child, Klaus, was placed in the custody of his maternal grandmother. Klaus found it difficult to discuss openly these recent losses, but did acknowledge that his present living arrangement was unsatisfactory. "My Oma is old, and is very moody. Sometimes she's really good to me, but then, for no reason, she can tell me to get outside and leave her alone. But when I do go outside, there's nothing for me to do."

Klaus's interests are of a fairly solitary nature. He expresses an abiding curiosity in the way the world works and spends a good deal of time exploring chemistry, physics, and electronics books. In addition, he wages a constant struggle to understand his nation's history, perhaps looking there for some explanation as to his own predicament. During a class visit to the countryside of West Germany, while his classmates were off exploring the nearby woods and rivers, Klaus would patiently root around the remains of an old Second World War bunker, unearthing scraps of jeeps and other war debris. He would remain engrossed in this task for hours, occasionally to be joined by the other boys who, on realizing the meagerness of the "find," soon lost interest. Yet Klaus would stay on, piecing together clues to a moment in his nation's history.

I'd say the Third Reich was the most important part of German history. There was a television show on a while ago about the last two weeks of Hitler's life, of how he killed himself. I like to watch shows like that. I think in a lot of the world there's a hate against us Germans; and maybe pity, too, because of what my country did during the war. Especially what we did to the Jews. That was terrible I know. . . . But Hitler also gave Germans work, and we can't forget that. Before he came to power, there was so much unemployment and uncertainty. And he got highways built, houses and monuments. I'm not sure I know the history that well, but I think the war started after Hitler's invasion of Poland and then of Russia. My father feels he should have attacked England first, and then gone on to Russia. Then we might have won the war.

I sometimes try to imagine what it would be like if we had won. It's hard. Maybe England, Poland, and even Moscow might belong to us. It would be better, too, because we'd have the East Mark, which is now in the DDR and Poland. There's a lot of good farmland there, so we could feed and take better care of our people. But I also feel it would be hard to maintain such a large Germany. I guess a united Germany would be good enough.

It seemed that Klaus was often wondering how his country, his life would be different, maybe even better, if at a certain moment in history things had gone another way. Many of the children with whom I spoke resent this burden of the past; they are tired of being reminded over and over again—either by the various "sights" within their own city or by the (still) angry comments of other Europeans—of their nation's (and by extension, their) particular "badness." One way Klaus has of dealing with such feelings is to "undo" that reality through fantasy. He makes rather explicit connections between his fantasies for his nation and his private, familially oriented wishes. "If we won the war, then Germany wouldn't be divided, and Berlin would still be the capital. Maybe then there'd be more jobs, and better jobs. I don't know, but things might be so different. Maybe my family would be richer, and we'd have a small house in the mountains in Bavaria. . . . Sometimes I think how different it all could be."

These fantasies are often followed up by an acknowledgment of grim reality. "Well, the war was terrible. And we did lose. And the killing of the Jews will never leave us. We will never be able to forget it." It is difficult, this feeling of responsibility so many children feel. Most of them are taught in school that they are in no way responsible, so it is even more surprising to see how common it is for children to feel the claim a painful past lays on them. Still, they often resent and struggle to reject these feelings. "I feel we've done enough to try to make up for it. Leave it alone now. We're a generation that had nothing to do with it. Germany is different now; yet no one wants to see that." Yet, who then to blame?

Back in West Berlin, Klaus would usually determine the place of our meetings. Generally he chose museums or historic landmarks: the

Reichstag; the Brandenburg Gate; the Plötzensee Memorial (dedicated to the soldiers implicated in the Officer's Plot of 1944, and later executed); or along the Wall itself, at one of the many "viewing platforms" erected by the city, from which one can gaze over the Wall into the well-patrolled no-man's-land of automatic shooting devices, guard towers, land mines, and, farther on, the city of East Berlin. It appeared that Klaus sought out such places because they stimulated him in his pursuit to know himself and his nation. On some level he was aware that his personal fate was inextricably bound up with the fate of his country. Indeed, as he spoke of his city, of the war, or of East Berlin, I could hear the way certain of his intimate fears, insecurities, and struggles were worked into those words.

Some good and some bad came out of the war. On the one hand, we won the friendship of France, England, and America. On the other hand, Berlin is an occupied city and our country is divided, with the Russians occupying part of it. That's not good for us. I think it's an advantage for the other countries, but not for us. Because in Germany there was a lot of industry and important people; and the occupying powers got them.

See after the war Germany was divided into four zones. The Russians cut themselves off from the others, and took over their zone. The Allies gave us back our government, but the Russians stayed. People began to leave the GDR because they knew they'd lose their freedom under the Russians. . . . I don't think it's fair that there are two Germanys. I think we should be reunited, since we're all German. But that will never happen, because West Germany wants all of Germany to be like us; and the GDR wants all of Germany to be like *them.*

More so than for his peers, the division of what was once a unified Germany generates in Klaus a feeling of loss. He is unable or unwilling to clearly disassociate the GDR from his own country and sees their forced division as cruel and unnecessary. In addition, he links hopes of a better, more just life with the reunification of the two German states, although he remains fairly pessimistic as to the likelihood of that. In some respects the separation of families caused by the establishment of two German states echoes the devastating losses suffered by Klaus in his own family. He speaks of the German people somewhat idealistically, as a people whose qualities transcend political and geographical barriers. "I'd say Germans are pretty much the same here or over there. They're great fighters, hardworking, faithful, and able to work together." Unlike many of his peers, Klaus is not so eager to heap blame on East Germany. Rather, he sees both nations on either side of the Wall as closely related—divided not by the inherent badness of one or the other but by the arbitrariness of history and, more specifically, by the vindictive conquering nations. If Germany was a family, it was a family torn apart by outsiders: the Soviet Union and the Allies. Klaus most openly expresses fear and distrust of the former, although his comments on the latter—the United States in particular—register a keen ambivalence. Some of these feelings came tumbling out on a particularly cold November day as Klaus and I emerged from the museum called "Haus am Checkpoint Charlie," its contents a gloomy chronicle of the history surrounding the building of the Berlin Wall, told in frequently moving human terms. It quite clearly touched Klaus; and, as we made our way from the museum toward the Wall, some twenty yards away, past the Checkpoint Charlie Imbiss (where knockwurst, bockwurst, bratwurst, bouletten, and pommes frites all go for a low price), and climbed the stairs to the observation platform overlooking the busy checkpoint, he mulled over all he had seen.

This Wall! Diese scheiss Mauer. It reminds us of our history and of what has happened to Germany—that there is now a part of this country called the GDR, where there are no human rights. Where there are hundreds of killing machines along the border. We heard in school about some revolt over there, in 1958 [he is referring to the June 17, 1953, work stoppages]. The Germans there had to fight against Russian tanks. All because of the building of the Wall and the loss of freedom, and because it was so hard to get food and other things. It's terrible. But I also think the occupying powers could have done more to stop the building of the Wall. I'm not against them, but I think they must have agreed to it, or at least permitted it to be built. I don't know why they would let that happen.

I'm afraid of the Russians. They have all of East Germany; and I know they still want all of Berlin, too. Russia is a regime, not a democracy, and the people suffer there. There is no freedom of the press; and they do have unemployment, but the press can't say anything about it. People can only say what's allowed. And if someone votes against the Party, they go to jail.

The Americans were totally different; they let us build up after the war. But they still occupy us, which is bad; though they say it's a defense against the East. Maybe. But no one should be occupied; each should have his own country. And the government should be for everyone. We have so many demonstrations here in Berlin. I don't like some of them, but they are important, because everyone has the right to say his opinion. But even if it's not free over there, there isn't a true democracy here, as there is always a person in charge, and every wish of every citizen can't be fulfilled. I think the best would be no government.

But if there is government, it should take from the rich and give to the poor; and it should be sure some jobs get paid what they deserve. That's the way it's supposed to be over there, in the DDR. Here, we hear that the DDR is socialist. I think it is, "in Prinzip." Over there they say that the farmers and workers are kings. But from what I've heard, that's not true. The SED [Socialist Unity party] runs things there; and if you don't agree with them, you have a lot of trouble. The workers just have to follow orders, like they do here.

Here, Klaus's criticism of the East is not expressed in order to better illuminate the "goodness" of the West. In fact, he embraces certain socialist ideals (as he understands them), and with those in mind he criticizes the two societies on either side of the Wall.

"I think the biggest problem in my country is the rich and poor here. The officials talk of the economic trouble we're in. But I ask myself; how much do bank presidents or state officials earn? They could earn less and give the extra money to the poor. We must help the poor, the people out of work. We must make more working places, provide more jobs. But our politicians don't seem to want to do this, or maybe they can't. Another big problem is the unions; they're always demanding bigger paychecks. But the more workers get paid, the more expensive products get, and the more workers have to get paid. It just keeps getting worse.

Now, if I were chancellor, I'd put pressures on the unions. And I'd try and help the poor more. Then I'd try to reduce the cold war between us and the DDR. But not like Schmitt, who speaks to the leaders there. I'd want to speak with the citizens and let *them* know what we think here, and to tell them what's wrong with their society, and maybe figure out how we can help each other.

Yet Klaus is not sure that his hopes can be fulfilled by the system in which he presently lives. "Sometimes I think we need a second Führer to do what Hitler did before the war—to provide employment, without making the mistakes Hitler made. But today no politician could do that. There are too many small political groups, and a Führer, if he is to be effective, needs a great mass of people behind him."

As he considers various alternatives to the status quo, Klaus turns again to the GDR, only this time not in criticism. Despite his rather piecemeal understanding of life in the GDR, or perhaps because of it, that country represents not only that which is "bad," but also suggests possibilities for happiness and security so seriously lacking in Klaus's own life.

> The best thing about the DDR is that children there are well taken care of [betreut]. They have the FDJ [Freie Deutsche Jugend—Free German Youth] and the Pioneers. If I were there, I'd get into a Pioneer group. I'm interested in electronics, and I could probably find a group there with similar interests, and with whom I could spend time. There's a better chance to learn more. Here in West Berlin there are no groups like that. Some kids here go crazy; there's nothing to do. They play on the street, but they don't learn. There are too many children who are alone, and who watch too much television. I'd love to start a Pioneer group here—but without the political side, the way it is over there. Maybe I'd have nature excursions and discussions.

In addition to his search for a feeling of security and well-being, Klaus has repeatedly indicated that he is also looking for meaning. In so doing, he draws on facts and fantasies of his immediate political surroundings and fashions his own blueprint for establishing this meaning.

> Something else they have over there that we don't have here is enthusiasm [Begeisterung]. There the people get excited about political leaders, and the army is very visible. In many ways the politics there *is* Hitler's politics—both in a good and a bad way. Here in West Berlin we are apathetic, indifferent [abgestumpft]. There's nothing for people here to attach themselves to. I feel there's a loss of the soul here [ein seelischer Verlust]; there should be a large group for all of Germany, so that everyone can join in and talk. Before the capitulation, at the end of the war, Germany was full of enthusiasm. Yet afterward, all feeling of honor was lost, disappeared. Since then, no one has been able to build up this spirit again.
>
> I believe people must believe in something larger. They need hope,

and a leader. In those days, people could hold onto something, someone [konnten an jemanden festhalten]. Yet so many people feel forgotten today, and the connections between the people and the government are so weak, that it's hard for people to feel they're part of something larger than themselves. And they begin to lose hope.

As with most children, Klaus's close scrutiny of his surroundings is an occasion for voicing not only perceptive observations about the political world but certain private hopes and wishes that are tethered to these external circumstances, framed by them. As he gazes at the Wall, Klaus is indeed gazing farther—at a nation's, as well as his own, past, as well as its uncertain future. Klaus continues:

> As for me, I'm proud of my country. I think everyone is proud of his country. There's love of country [Vaterlandliebe], and it's a real shame when someone does not have it. It means we have a connection to our country. It would help if Germany were not divided, because then we could say, Germany remains Germany [Deutschland bleibt Deutschland]. If we weren't divided, we could have a better conscience, feel better about ourselves. With the division, we are always reminded of the war and always hear bad things about ourselves. Also, if we weren't divided, Germany would be bigger, there'd be less tension, and Berlin would no longer be an island.

After talking with a child like Klaus, the distinction between a child's political beliefs, moral concerns, and "inner life" appears increasingly arbitrary. Klaus *is* his nation's history, just as he is the child of a particularly unfortunate working class couple, filled with sadness and confusion, as well as a desire to make sense of this life using what clues are available to him: the ebb and flow of history as it is embodied in his city, his education, his family.

The last day that I saw Klaus, we wandered around his neighborhood. It was a clear, early summer day, the air no longer choked with the smoke of thousands of burning coal stoves. The apartment houses there have fallen into disrepair. Because of the haste with which housing was built immediately after the war, cheaper materials were used, and less care taken. Consequently, many of these buildings appear far older than their years, and resemble similar houses in East Berlin. West Berlin is indeed a glittery monument to western capitalism, but it has its pockets of ordinariness and decay where the hard-pressed make their lives. Klaus and I were speaking of our plans; I mentioned my hopes of writing a book; he, too, had hopes of writing a book, and his subject was already well established: "I would like to write a novel about a family, one that is dramatic and very harsh. Without a happy end."

5 | The Children of East Berlin

In school we learn that the Wall was built to keep out spies from the West, who wanted to ruin our country. Maybe that's true, and sometimes I worry that the FRG or America will start a war with us. But I also hear other things. Last week I saw a television program from the West about the border. I learned a lot of things I never heard here. It really makes me sick, the border. You can see it behind our school; it's really well protected. There are always lots of guards there, and this television program said they even have automatic shooting machines. To shoot *us* if we try to leave!

And then they tell us how wonderful it is here. But they know if people had the chance, most would leave. Why else is the border there? If I could, I think I would go there. But I don't know if I would want to live in the West; I'd be worried about all the unemployment and "Kaos" there. But we have relatives over there, and I would like to visit them sometimes. I know they're supposed to be our enemy, and I think some of them are. But not my aunt.

What the government doesn't understand is that most people would just want to be able to visit over there, and then come back here. That's what I want to do. I'd still live here; this is my home.—Dirk

Unlike their peers in West Berlin, children in East Berlin, such as twelve-year-old Dirk, are caught in the crossfire between socialist rhetoric and western ideology as it is represented on television. With very little guidance they are forced to evaluate these conflicting messages and to come to some kind of understanding of what is indeed a complicated political reality. They, too, must draw on various aspects of their experience and imagination in making their political and moral assessments. Yet they live with a radically different ideology which fosters a different relationship between the individual and the state, and they have ready access to a wide range of information about the other Germany through television, including the opportunity to view themselves and their nation through the eyes of the presumed "enemy." Hence, they are in a position to make observations quite different from those made by children in West Berlin.

In his statement Dirk raises issues that are of consequence to many of the children with whom I spoke, and he makes clear the various sources of information on which they rely. In school and through other official representatives of the regime, children learn of the protective significance of the Wall. The "enemy," as Dirk points out, lies directly to the other side, and is a constant threat to the city's and the state's internal security. Yet the reality of the Wall as these children experience it (recall Jörg's run-in with police in a cemetery adjoining the Wall) and as it is portrayed by relatives from "over there," along with western television programs, suggests other reasons for its construction. And an understanding of the Wall as a means of preventing escape forces children to look carefully at their own government. Not just a reminder of a brutal past, nor an indication of the "badness" of the West, the Wall forces children to turn a critical eye on their own system—something young people do with varying degrees of enthusiasm or reluctance. Children are very much struck—and horrified by—the fact that their own government may have its guns turned on *them*.

Nonetheless, as Dirk's words indicate, many children express a marked ambivalence toward the West. On the negative side is the realization that it could turn its military aggression on the East; and it is riddled with economic insecurity, compounded by the insecurity bred by the all-too-frequent West Berlin street demonstrations, which are displayed on East Berlin television screens. Yet, as with West Berlin's children, these young people have family "over there"—a powerful argument against the "Feindbild" (enemy picture) of the West that is so ubiquitous in the German Democratic Republic. They, too, recognize and are confused by the pull of family ties that works like an undertow against the insistent rhetoric emphasizing national differences and reminds young people of the connections between the two nations.

Finally, and very importantly, Dirk asserts his need for a certain kind of freedom—to travel and satisfy a deep curiosity about the West—while maintaining that his home does lie in East Berlin. Perhaps even more than for West Berlin children, the family and neighborhood are of great significance for these kids. Caught by virtue of television technology *between* ideological worlds, they are often left not knowing what to believe. And family may offer much-needed certainties and room for trust.

Television may exert the most powerful influence on the developing political and national views of these East Berlin children. Whereas young people in the West must work at acquiring a genuine understanding of life in the East, East Berlin young people are exposed daily to the whole range of western life and thought as it is portrayed on television. Although the viewing of "west television" was severely discouraged in the late sixties and early seventies, authorities have quietly conceded defeat in this regard. And they have gone one step further. "Today new housing projects have communal antennas to eliminate the need for a forest of individual roof aerials. Among the advantages, this prevents embarrassment for party members, who would otherwise have to put up their own antennas."[1]

For many children it is this media experience that proves so influential as they try to figure out where they fit into a particular national and moral landscape. Yet if television viewing manages to undermine or enhance the child's allegiance to his own nation, it is not due solely to the persuasive power of the medium. Those western television broadcasts are viewed within a specific political, social, and familial context, and the information children receive from those programs is then held up to the light of their experience at home, at school, or on the streets. Television may then confirm certain observations of these young people, or its message may be contradicted by their experience. For most children this process of comparing the various sources of their information about their political world is, if nothing else, terribly confusing. One fifteen-year-old boy told me: "When I was ten, I became very interested in television news and used to watch a west station and our station every day, so that I could compare them. But it got very confusing, because I was sure the West wasn't always lying, but I never had any way of really knowing what the truth was. Now I don't watch news at all; I've just given up trying to figure it out. I know our government is always telling lies, and I just have no way of finding out for myself what is true and what isn't."

Although young children appear not to be in a position to question seriously what they are taught in school (and are, in fact, enthusiastic about much of it), by the time they reach eleven or twelve they have begun to notice discrepancies between rhetoric and experience and to question much that they had previously taken for granted. For many young people there are several possible responses to the ensuing uncertainty: they can throw themselves wholeheartedly into the regime values and be labeled by themselves and others as "linientreu" or "überzeugt" (truly committed); they can slip into the despair of cynicism; they can continue to struggle with the uncertainties and ambiguities inherent in their circumstances; or they can, as do many, take leave of that world and retreat to the more tangible and reliable world of family and friends. As well, children and young people are increasingly being drawn to the church. As in other East European countries, the polarity of church and state has acquired real moral significance, with the church becoming the repository of values and beliefs no longer accepted or honored by the state.

Most of my young informants were by no means "überzeugt." Of course, as an outsider from the West, I was hardly in a position to meet with children who might be, or who came from families with a strong investment in their nation's political life, and their own personal political future. As Hans's mother indicated (chapter 3), they would have their own reasons to avoid me. Still, although there are no questionnaire studies documenting public opinion in the GDR, numerous unofficial sources indicate that no more than 5 percent of the nation's populace could be considered deeply supportive of regime values.

The children with whom I was able to speak were, by and large, wrestling with the ambivalence that was their response to their national and personal predicament. Their statements often veered radically and unpredictably between the assurance of rhetoric and their far less comfortable personal doubts. Their words reflected an abiding unease in discussing anything political, and their drawings also were influenced by this discomfort with the political world. Frequently, when given the opportunity to draw "something I should know about your country," they steered clear of explicitly political themes that were so appealing to their West Berlin peers, and focused on domestic, less anxiety-provoking images. Many children drew pictures of their homes—real or ideal. Rather than capturing their imaginations, political life had become for many something to avoid. This appears to reflect not only a disinterest in such topics but also the fear of addressing those particular issues in public, especially with a relative stranger. Experience has taught them that the political world can be a tricky, sometimes dangerous place in which to maneuver. Over time, many of these children would let down some of their guard, yet they often expressed their deepest feelings through humor or sarcasm. They have already learned to say obliquely what they fear to say directly.

Although the presence of the Wall stimulates the historical curiosity of many of these children, they are better equipped (ideologically) to put some distance between themselves and that ugly national past. History texts and rhetoric alike insist on the clear separation between the GDR and its predecessor, the Third Reich: out of the ashes of fascism arose a new socialist German state. Children accept this feat of historical dissociation with varying degrees of assurance.

> I know there was one German nation once. It was fascist, and run by Hitler. He was a terrible man, and he was supported by the fascists. They wanted to take over the world, and killed the Jews and destroyed a lot of Europe. After the liberation, we kicked out all the fascists from the GDR. Now, they live in West Germany, or some of them are in South America. But here we have a socialist state, and the reason we have the Wall is to keep the fascists out. Maybe they will try to destroy us, just like they did other countries during the war.

To be sure, this twelve-year-old boy's words are laced with the standard rhetoric of East German life, and it is difficult to know where polemic becomes part of personal conviction (a question that is at the heart of this study). Yet to dismiss these words as "mere" rhetoric is a mistake, for they manage to convey a certain historical truth and offer consolation as well. In many respects, the GDR's postwar efforts at denazification were far more stringent and successful than those of the western Allies in what came to be West Germany. When speaking of the war and the crimes perpetrated by members of Hitler's Reich, East Berlin children rarely implicated themselves in that time. Rather than acknowledge their connection to the past, as did many West Berlin children, they often appeared more comfortable with the "we-they" dichotomy (GDR citizens/fascists) stressed in the school.

Naturally, the task I faced when speaking with these children was to peer beneath the rhetoric—to try to establish when it was heartfelt, when it was simply spoken in the interest of self-protection, or when it was used with a certain political and psychological discrimination, a convenient means of dealing with specific troubling questions. One such troubling issue: in spite of the official insistence on the dissociation of the GDR from the past, East Germany is full of "fascists"—the grandparents and parents of these children with whom I spoke. And children here, as in West Berlin, hear stories at home that invariably confuse the issues, often contradicting the official version of the war and its aftermath.

> They keep saying we had nothing to do with the war—that the fascists started it, and that they all live over there now, or something. But my Opa (grandfather) lives here, near us on Oderbergerstrasse. And he fought in the war, with the Germans under Hitler, or the fascists. I don't know if he was a fascist or not, but he did have to fight. And that means the people who fought aren't just "over there." There was one Germany once, and we come from there too. My Opa has friends over there still. I don't know though . . . I don't think my Opa is a fascist like we learn in school. Maybe the really bad ones *are* over there.

For twelve-year-old Anna the confrontation of family history and official rhetoric forces her to pause and reflect on the veracity of both. State truths are rarely completely discarded; and children are left in a quandary when an acceptance of rhetoric forces them to question certain family truths. In Anna's case it is perhaps easier to accept much of the official "truth" that will allow her to get her grandfather off the hook and to direct blame and responsibility for the war on the fascists "over there."

Whereas many West Berlin children referred frequently and poignantly to the Second World War, these East Berlin youngsters appeared less troubled by and less interested in that past. This is ironic in some respects, as so much more attention is paid in the schools to that history; it is, after all, the raison d'être for the formation of the GDR. Children are required at an early age to visit various concentration camps, and in this and other ways are constantly reminded of the horror of the war.

Yet the Wall, for most of these children, is something that affects them most decisively *now;* and it affects them in ways quite different from the ways it does their western counterparts. Most children appear to go through two significant steps of awareness of the Wall's significance. When they are quite young they generally accept the official explanation for the Wall's presence. Only later, as they have begun to make observations somewhat discrepant to rhetoric, and usually after they have had a liberal dose of west television, do they reassess the Wall. This new recognition is frequently accompanied by a mixed set of feelings: confusion, hurt, outrage, and fear. Twelve-year-old Gritt gives an account of her shifting perceptions of the Wall:

> We learn in school that the Wall was built to protect us from capitalists

who want to invade our socialist land. I used to believe that completely. When I was in the third grade, we visited a monument to a border guard who was killed by someone from the West. He was supposed to be like a hero for us, and I remember I thought he was. A lot of the kids did. But after a while I thought differently. Have you ever seen the Wall? If it was meant to keep *them* out, the land mines, soldiers, and self-shooting machines would be on the *other* side. Now, whenever I hear on west television that someone has escaped, I cheer for them.

During one of my visits to Gritt's home I joined her family for a light dinner of eggs, sausage, and bread in front of the television. So many of my visits to these families took place within the flicker of television, and this night was no exception. As we ate and talked, we heard a western newscaster provide the details of a recent escape from the GDR over the North Sea. Gritt, as well as her mother and stepfather, broke into delighted laughter. Later her mother explained:

> I try to make it as easy for Gritt as I can. I know she has to live in this society, and it would be better if I could tell her with some conviction that I like it here. The truth is, I don't hate it; there are good sides to life here that I try to explain to Gritt. But I don't *want* her to feel it's fine to shoot down people who only want to leave this place. Besides, even if I didn't say anything, she has begun to make up her own mind about things. And television has a lot to do with that. I remember the first time she heard about someone getting shot at the Wall; there was some story in the news from "over there" and of course they made it very dramatic. Well, it *was* terrible. And Gritt got very upset; she didn't say anything at first, and then she kept wanting to know *why* they did it. And I didn't know what to say. How do you tell a child that her own government shoots its people? Now she really likes to hear about people who do make it. And so do I.

On another occasion, as Gritt and a few of her friends were taking me on a walking tour of their neighborhood, I asked her about that time described by her mother.

> I'll never forget it. That was when I really began to feel like they were lying to us here. Up until then I just thought the Wall was there to keep "them" out, like I told you. But that night on the west news they told about this man who was killed when he tried to get over the Wall. There was one picture of him lying there in "no man's land," dead I think. And

just because he wanted to go to the West. They should have just let him go; but they won't let any of us go. *That's* why the Wall is there!

As with Matthias in West Berlin, who recalls the first time his father took him to the Wall, and Brigitte, who was "witness" (from her side of the Wall) to an escape attempt, this televised moment was for Gritt a crystallizing experience of sorts. Suddenly her world was no longer operating as she had been led to believe. This event, followed by other similar events, led Gritt (and others like her) to the frightening and disillusioning observation that her nation is, in part, her adversary—one that can deal rather brutally with its internal opponents.

Children in East Berlin learn to be very careful observers, finding out early what to say and to whom. They know that such watchfulness is their best defense in a world where people must separate personal opinion from state opinion, and where forgetting that distinction can be a dangerous mistake. I recall a conversation with twelve-year-old Stephan, who made this all too clear: "Sometimes it's easy to see who I have to watch out for. Usually it's better not to say anything around a stranger, but some strangers are more dangerous than others. The first thing I look for is a [Socialist Unity] party pin. I can usually spot that from a long way off, since they wear them on their coats. You really have to be careful around party people—that's what my parents tell me."

As Stephan and I walked along the crumbling back streets of East Berlin, in the district of Prenzlauer Berg, I noticed his ability to keep talking while surveying his surroundings carefully. And this was not a defensive maneuver peculiar to Stephan. These children are as watchful in school, in conversation with teachers or leaders of the assorted youth groups, or in the way they compare and evaluate West German versus East German news programs. Such care had a direct influence on the way in which I carried out my fieldwork, as children only felt at ease when they were at home among trusted family members or on the streets, away from any potentially threatening listeners. Whenever we would stop in an ice cream parlor or a bookstore, our conversations always became more constrained, guarded, and uncertain.

Many of the conflicting feelings children have toward the state are generated by experiences in the school. In the GDR the classroom is the state's primary battleground for the hearts and minds of its children; and education is conceived as a "class weapon in the struggle with implacable foes."[2] In its efforts to win the allegiance of young people, the state "encourages" them to become members of the various youth organizations made available to them in and out of the school. The primary means of involving young people in the political and economic life of the GDR is the Free German Youth (Freie Deutsche Jugend-FDJ). Founded on March 7, 1946, the FDJ is officially regarded as a "reliable helper"[3] of the SED [Socialist Unity party]; units of the FDJ are found in schools, factories, collective farms, the military, and in residential neighborhoods. All young people between the ages of fourteen and twenty-five are eligible for membership. The junior organization of the FDJ is the Ernst Thälmann Pioneer organization, for children between six and fourteen years. It includes the Young Pioneers, for ages six to eight. In an effort to demonstrate the popularity of these organizations among young people, the state has provided figures indicating that out of a total of approximately 3 million citizens between fourteen and twenty-five years, almost 2 million were members of FDJ in 1974. Of children between the ages of six and fourteen, 96 percent were members of the two Pioneer organizations.[4]

Yet figures on enrollment in political organizations do not provide a clue as to why young people join them, nor do they shed light on the effect such membership has on personal attitudes and beliefs. For many younger children such groups serve an important function, somewhat similar to what West Berlin's Klaus had in mind: they give children the opportunity to learn new skills, to play games, and to feel as though they are part of a community. In this respect one might liken an organization such as the Pioneers to a western youth group such as the Boy Scouts. Yet, as extensions of the state, these groups have a very clear purpose: to socialize children as members of a *particular* nation. And there are indeed children for whom such groups are a positive experience, at least initially. Eleven-year-old Sybilla explained the appeal her Thälmann Pioneer group has for her:

> Everyone I know joins the Pioneers; I never thought I wouldn't join. You just do; it's part of school. And I like it most of the time because I get to be with my friends, and if I didn't join there'd be nothing to do after school. We do different things: sometimes we play games like "maneuvers," where it's capitalists against socialists. That's fun. Or we'll collect clothes or other stuff for the poor children of Poland, or other needy countries like Vietnam or Kampuchea. A lot of the time we meet and discuss political things. It's okay, I guess; but when I'm with

my friends we don't talk about that stuff. Most of my friends aren't so enthusiastic [begeistert] about it. Sometimes I am, but not always.

As Sybilla's words suggest, she has begun to acquire a sense of her nation's political priorities and is able to discuss them freely. Games like "socialists versus capitalists" reinforce children's awareness of an ideological struggle that is of paramount importance to the state. In addition, children learn the names of nations considered friendly with theirs; and though they are just names for many of them, it is significant that they are becoming familiar with the so-called socialist or communist world early on, and are learning to associate notions of friendship or peaceableness with those words *socialist* and *communist*.

Yet what do her words reveal about her emotional response to the overriding political orientation of these youth groups and of her education in general? Toward the end of her statement Sybilla does touch on her occasional disinterest in and dissatisfaction with the blatant political content of her school experience. Her drawings always veered sharply away from the political and instead revealed her personal interests: she drew horses a good deal, reflecting her love of animals and her hopes of becoming a veterinarian. Only much later was Sybilla willing to be more explicit in her expression of ambivalence toward school life and in her admission of confusion—a feeling prominent in her peers.

> Sometimes I do get tired of it. Always politics. My mother says I just have to try to learn it if I want to be a veterinarian. I think she gets tired of it too. But I have to pay attention, I know that. Sometimes I listen to west radio, or watch west television, though. Then I get really confused. I know one of them [West or East] must be lying. But I'm never *sure*. I'll ask my mother, or talk with my friends; but sometimes I just have to go on my own feeling. I have to trust my feelings since there's no other way of being sure.

In the school children also learn unofficial lessons that seriously undermine the firm sense of allegiance to the tenets of socialist ideology that is intended for them. Repeatedly I heard stories about the child (there always seemed to be at least one) in this or that class who made the mistake of contradicting the teacher once too often, or of disagreeing with a specific interpretation of historical or current events (often a reflection of parental complaints heard at home), or whose parents happened to be active church members. Frequently he would suffer specific consequences (albeit varying in severity) that were a sharp reminder, not only to him but to his classmates, of the price one pays for violating ideological propriety.

Following is an account by twelve-year-old Annette, culled from numerous conversations in which she spoke of her experiences and those of her elder brother subsequent to her mother's "escape" to West Berlin. These conversations took place in West Berlin, where Annette had arrived five months earlier, two years after her mother's departure from East Berlin. Of course, this fact makes Annette an exceptional member of my sample, although much of what she told me could be heard in East Berlin as well. Yet hers is one of those stories that effectively dramatize an experience common to others. Her words are a poignant reminder not only of the desperation particular parents may feel, but, more to the point, of the painful consequences faced by children on account of their parents' particular "sins" against ideological purity.

Annette's mother had been a schoolteacher in East Berlin, and her husband a minor bureaucrat. Annette lived with them and her fifteen-year-old brother Andre in the Mitte district of East Berlin. Two and a half years prior to my conversations with Annette, her mother had successfully petitioned to be allowed to visit her ailing mother in West Berlin. Once there, she simply stayed, assuming that the state would ultimately release her family to rejoin her. Two years later it did, after putting the three of them through a good deal of emotional and material hardship. Says Annette:

> I didn't know my mother was going to leave us. My Oma was sick in the West, and so I knew Mutti was going to visit her. But I thought she was coming back. She never told us she was leaving, but after her time to return was over, I knew it. And my father told us what she did. I couldn't believe she'd just go without saying goodbye.
>
> Once she left, things got bad for my brother and me—especially for Andre. Teachers started treating me differently; they didn't call on me so much and I would get lower grades for the same work I always did. One teacher kept asking me what kind of a mother would leave her family like that, and I never knew what to say. But it wasn't my fault that she left.
>
> But the worst part was the other kids. For a while they didn't know where my mother was. It was really hard for me; I kept making up stories to tell my friends, because they all wanted to know where she was. After a while I was running out of things to say. And then they found out. And

a lot of them started to stay away from me like there was something wrong with me. I hated that.

It was worse for my brother. He was so upset; he used to be a good student, and then *his* grades dropped too. Just because my mother went to the West. He would fight with his teachers, and then they didn't let him take his Abitur. So he dropped out. I would talk with him, and he would tell me why they did this to us. But after we talked, I still didn't know what to think. And I was always sad; my mother was gone and everything was going wrong. Vati [Father] just kept saying we had to be patient.

Up until then I think I was pretty happy. I liked school enough; I used to love it when the soldiers came to school, or when we would visit the barracks. I was "begeistert" I guess. A lot of kids are then. But then when you get to be eleven or twelve, it's not so good anymore. . . .

I think many people would leave if they could travel to the West. At first they'd all leave, because they'd be afraid the border would be closed again. But then if it wasn't, they'd return. I don't think my mother would, though; she was a nervous wreck over there. When she got here, it was like she was reborn.

Annette's mother agreed with her daughter's last statement, and she spoke somewhat tersely about her decision to leave as she did:

I knew I had to leave that place. It's terribly hard for any teacher there—day in and day out to keep personal thoughts and feelings buried while mouthing official ideology. I was an English and sport teacher, and I hated to see how over-stressed sport is over there. At least once a month someone would come into the classroom and get the kids to do pushups, situps, or check the size of their hands, their shoulders—and decide what sport they'd be good at. If they had "potential," they would then be trained; and although parents are asked, they rarely refuse, as a refusal is tantamount to denying the state's needs. Everything for the state! I just couldn't take that.

I had thought about fleeing to the West for two years before I actually did. And I don't think I was certain I'd do it until I was in West Berlin. I know how hard it was for the children, but I felt I had no choice. Children are too easy to get information out of; and I couldn't risk that.

One can imagine the difficulty a young child faces when her mother inexplicably leaves and remains out of sight for two years; and of course

Annette's feelings toward her mother were decidedly mixed, with a generous dose of anger and a sense of betrayal. And it takes a certain kind of mother to be able to leave her family without a goodbye, knowing full well the adversity her decision will put them in. Yet such a decision may have been the only one possible, given the extreme difficulty of legally emigrating from the GDR. Annette undoubtedly struggles between asking how her mother could have left her like that and asking how her nation could make that her mother's only option. Turning on the state may make it easier for Annette to spare her mother her anger and resentment. But she also has genuine cause for directing that anger at the state. Certainly, most children do not share in Annette's experience; they will no doubt spend their lives in the GDR. Yet they see what happens to a girl like Annette, or to other children "guilty" of lesser indiscretions, and they learn, if not to be "linientreu," at least to be careful in their behavior and their associations.

What do children make of these problems encountered by certain of their peers? Annette's brother Andre often wondered whether his classmates avoided him out of a genuine conviction that he was ideologically suspect or whether they did so out of self-protectiveness. After speaking with a wide range of children, I would say that a majority of those young people over age eleven or twelve were beginning to distinguish political conviction from concern with personal safety. Most of them would avoid certain transgressors in the school in order to prevent their own academic, and later employment, difficulties. Twelve-year-old Hans Martin told me of his experience.

> There's a boy in my class; I've known him since the first grade. He's not a good friend, but he's not a bad kid. A couple of years ago we found out his parents are in the church and the peace movement. I don't really know; I never talk to him about it. I don't even remember how we found out. But the teachers aren't easy on him since then, and no one wants to be with him in school. Maybe some of the kids at first thought there was something wrong with him. But now I think most kids just don't want any trouble. They know he's not "bad," but it might be bad to hang around him.

The lesson learned under such circumstances is the same one that is learned when children hear of an escaping citizen being shot and killed at the Wall: the state (and its representatives: police, soldiers, Stasi members, even teachers) can be, in very significant respects, a dangerous adversary—capable of exercising its authority in a brutal and arbitrary manner. Certainly not all teachers are willing to penalize children for their various "slips" or for their efforts to express their opinions. Yet there are teachers who do this, either out of personal conviction or out of their own fears of political censure (which often means professional suicide). As they become more aware of this, children frequently acquire a bitter cynicism that underlies their motivation to become members of various political organizations such as the Pioneers or the FDJ. One thirteen-year-old boy told me, "I didn't think much about it when I joined the Young Pioneers. I liked my group; we did fun stuff. But sometimes I get sick of it all; only I won't quit. Everyone tells me it's better for me if I stay; I'll do better in school and I'll get a better job. No one has to tell me, though; I have eyes. So I act 'begeistert,' but I'm not. Nobody really is. I just keep going so nothing bad happens to me. I'll probably even join the FDJ."

There are yet other lessons that children attend to—lessons that have to do with economics and the distribution of wealth and privilege. Although children in any society do not have to look far to see who is being rewarded and why, they are occasionally assisted by the presence of something, or by a telling incident, that enables them to focus their developing regard for issues of equity and fairness. In the GDR this "something" might well be the system of Intershops—shops where East German citizens with western currency can buy western consumer items at marked-up prices. Established by the government as a means of bringing much-needed western currency into the state's coffers and to assuage consumer desires for western goods, the operation has backfired—leading to even greater consumer dissatisfaction and a heavily trafficked black market. In addition, the failure of the Intershops—from the point of view of the average person—has highlighted the inequities in a system that claims to have effectively diminished the significance of class differences and related allocation of privilege.

Like television, Intershops bring the average East German that much closer to certain realities of the West, while denying either experience or possession of those realities. The primary economic lesson here is that eastern currency, for which most citizens work very hard, is worthless when it comes to acquiring goods that really count. The Intershop is then a slap in the face—holding out the promise of "affluence" while scoffing at the means whereby most citizens would acquire a share in that affluence. In addition, it soon becomes clear who can afford those items on the terms set by the government. And as one begins to look around even more carefully, one sees the political and economic infrastructure that is a source of dissatisfaction and frustration for many—a system of formal and informal connections and influence peddling.

When I visited with children in East Berlin they frequently insisted that we head to the nearest Intershop to see what was available. They were keenly aware not only of the nature of items on sale but of their selling prices as well. One young mother expressed the surprise she had felt on learning of her son's familiarity with the Intershops. "When Sören was seven years old, he came home and said he wanted a skateboard. He knew we wouldn't be able to buy one here, yet he was fully informed as to how we might get one. 'You just have to go to the Intershop,' he said, 'and you have to change your money. If you're lucky, you change it three to one, and then the skateboard is cheap. If you're not lucky, you'll change it five to one.' I was so surprised; but when I thought about it, I wasn't. A child like Sören learns what is important to him."

My experience with children was similar; many of them expressed a keen desire to share in the wealth of their western neighbors. It was somewhat painful to witness their mixed feelings as they hovered over Intershop counters—full of desires, yet aware of the virtual impossibility of satisfying them. Such a situation leads children to ask why it is they are in such a position. Rather than consistently question the materialism of the West (which many children do), they often turn and look among themselves for the roots of their dissatisfaction. This leads to some very telling observations, such as that made by twelve-year-old Michael as we looked over the wide selection of popular jeans in the Intershop off Alexanderplatz:

> I come down here a lot—sometimes by myself and sometimes with my friends. And I wish I could buy something. My brother comes here and buys Marlboros, but I don't want cigarettes. Sometimes I start noticing the people who are buying stuff, and you can tell they have a lot of money. But in school they tell us there are no rich people here in the GDR. Well, maybe they're not really rich, like in the West, but they're a lot richer than my parents.
>
> But it's not just money you need. But *west* money. And you also need "Beziehungen" [connections]. My mother calls them Vitamin B. And some of these people here are really lucky; they have lots of connections. And it's not fair. My father also says it's not fair; but he tells me not to say anything.

The fact is, everything gets done faster with connections—from acquiring an apartment to buying a car (both of which normally require a wait of up to seven years). And connections often make the day-to-day life of an individual somewhat easier. One boy's father knows the butcher, and so choice cuts of meat are held aside for him and his family. A sixteen-year-old girl is friends with the daughter of a man who works in a record shop, and so she is assured early grabs on newly released records. And so on. As this is such a fact of life, it is often referred to with a laugh or a shrug. One joke making the rounds during my stay in Berlin went as follows. Question: What's the new form of punishment for breaking the law in the GDR? Answer: Seven years here without "Beziehungen." The joke, told frequently, elicited knowing and sometimes bitter laughter from young people and adults alike.

Yet there are political "Bezeihungen" as well; and it is these, and the privilege that goes to someone who has them, that arouses the ire of young people in particular. In warmer weather I would frequently take the trip down to the Müggelsee, on the southeast perimeter of the city, with one or several of the children I'd come to know. On a muggy weekend day thousands of East Berliners flock to the lake, seeking respite from their (more often than not) hot, cramped city apartments. At least this was certainly the case with my young informants. On one such occasion I was walking with twelve-year-old Karen from the last S-Bahn stop down toward the beach. On our way we were passing some lovely old one-family homes and villas, and she exclaimed:

> Look at these houses! They're so big, and beautiful. You want to know how you get to live here? Connections! A lot of the people here are the "Bonzen" [big shots] in the Party. I don't understand it. My Oma was a Trummelfrau; after the war she helped clear up the rubble, and worked like a horse. Now she gets two hundred marks a month, while the Bonzen do nothing and get one thousand marks a month. And they get to live here. That's not right. We always hear in school that there aren't any rich people here like in the West. But look at these villas!

Ironically, these children are equipped by virtue of their socialistic upbringing to scrutinize "society" in general, and their own society in particular, in terms of fairness and economic justice.

Aside from managing to make evident certain economic and political inequities in the system, the presence of Intershops highlights what, at times, appears to be a preoccupation with the material wealth of the West. With western currency and goods at such a premium, status comes to be defined in terms of the number and quality of connections one has with the

West. I have heard children argue as to whose grandmother or aunt in the West was wealthier and thereby more able to bring over specific coveted western items. In a child's life the presence of those prized connections often has a direct and occasionally a beneficial bearing on his personal life. One young boy I visited, eleven-year-old Christian, had a room full of western board games—the most striking of which was a *MAD* magazine game modeled along the lines of Monopoly, whereby the players' goal is to lose money. I noticed that when Christian and his friends would get together they would inevitably choose to meet at his home. By virtue of his western possessions he was much sought after in a manner that made even him pause to consider why. "I'm really lucky to have my aunt over in West Berlin; she's always bringing me things from over there, so it's not like I'm "stuck" here. I know I can't go to the West myself, but at least I can get some of the same things kids over there play with. I think I have more toys and stuff from over there than my other friends. I don't mind though, because they always come over here then! I like that." It is rather peculiar, the way in which the West—officially declared an ideological and military foe—becomes for many children a means of alleviating the everydayness of socialist life as well as a sure way of gaining a certain degree of status for themselves.

I have been talking about the lessons children learn in East Berlin as a prelude to discussing their various responses to both their own government and the one behind the Wall. Those lessons have to do with the nature of power—political and economic—and the manner in which it is exercised. I have tried to suggest that these lessons are taught sometimes in a vivid and dramatic manner, and often over the long haul of day-to-day experience. One dramatic reminder of the location of power in East Germany can be seen in the public parades and demonstrations intended to celebrate important national holidays ("Founding Day of the GDR" on October 7; the anniversary of the Russian Revolution, on November 7; or May Day). Attendance at such rallies is expected of children and their parents; schools are generally responsible for the participation of children, and places of work are required to send their own contingents of workers. It would be difficult to say that the resulting audience is enthusiastic. Although such demonstrations of the state's power are exciting to young children, who enjoy the music, displays of military might, and flag-waving, the responses of the eleven- and twelve-year-olds I knew were generally more mixed, if not downright negative. One child explained, "We're all supposed to go to the parades. Usually we have to meet at school, where they divide us into smaller groups. And then we are supposed to march over to Karl Marx Allee together. I hate it; it's so boring. Sometimes we can slip away down some side street, and then just go home. My parents don't care; they hate to go too. The problem is sometimes a teacher notices, and then you have trouble at school."

Children joked often of "freiwilliger Zwang," or "voluntary force," meaning, "you are forced to do something, yet must act as though you elect to do so." In fact, humor is especially important in this nation. Twelve-year-old Stephan, from whom we have already heard, told a joke while we were walking from his house down to the Museum Island at the heart of his city. As he spoke, he was sure to constantly check that we were quite alone. The joke concerns a competition of sorts between America, the GDR, and the Soviet Union. An American scientist is bragging: "We have an athlete who was in an accident and lost both his arms and legs. But we sewed them back on, and he has won a string of gold medals at the Olympics!" The Soviet scientist laughs and says: "That's nothing! One of our best scientists was in a terrible car wreck, and his head was cut off. We sewed it back on, and he recently won the Nobel Prize!" At this, the GDR scientist laughed and asserted: "Oh, that's nothing at all. We have a man here who not only lost his head in a car accident, but his brains leaked out as well. We sewed his head back on his body and replaced his brain with a soggy 'Brötchen' [bread roll], and he's *still* president of our country!" Although Stephan laughed at the conclusion of his joke, he also became especially nervous. The joke served as an effective expression of and release of some of his anger, but it also stimulated his anxiety at being overheard. Through jokes, sarcasm, even facial expressions, young people learn to convey what cannot be said directly. Metaphor becomes especially important; and it is no surprise that one of the most popular western films to be shown in East Berlin was *One Flew Over the Cuckoo's Nest*—a film concerned with life in the tightly controlled environment of a psychiatric hospital.

Yet it is not simply the GDR authorities who receive the brunt of this anger. What everyone knows, and what is made abundantly clear at certain public rallies, where Soviet military equipment rumbles along Karl Marx Allee for what seems an interminable amount of time, is that the Soviet Union pulls the strings here. And although the GDR is by and large hated by citizens of other Eastern Bloc countries for its apparent willingness to please the Soviet Union, the feeling of many people here is that they will tolerate what they cannot fight (partly because resistance appears futile and partly because the GDR has the highest standard of living in the Eastern Bloc)—while maintaining a personal resistance revealed in humor and muttered complaints. This resistance has even been officially acknowledged in the GDR, where there have been complaints about anti-Soviet remarks by Pioneer members.[5]

Unlike their peers in the West, who are often prompted by the Wall to criticism of the East, children in East Berlin reserve their bitterest diatribes not for the West but for the Soviet Union. Yes, they are willing to and capable of critiquing aspects of life in the West. Nevertheless, the Wall and the system it represents force many young people to look farther to the east. Many feel the same as young Stephan:

> We learn Russian in school because the Soviet Union is our "brother land," so to speak. And their language is an international language, like English. By "brother land," I guess they mean there's a sort of alliance between them and us—like the Warsaw Pact. And also because they freed us from the Nazis. But I don't think they feel like brothers at all. For me they are totally different people from us; and I don't even want them here. I sometimes think they even look different from us, though I might not recognize one if I saw him on the street out of uniform. I don't feel close to them at all.

That "so to speak" is important. When children spoke to me using ideologically correct terminology, they would frequently follow up with that short phrase, as if to say that "this is what I've been told to say, but there is another side." In addition, children frequently prefaced their responses to many of my questions by asking, "Do you want my opinion or the state's?" Many adults and older children have mentioned that the incessant government claims—in school, the media, on the ever-present placards and posters—of Soviet-GDR brotherhood start to sound false because of the stridency with which they are expressed. "If we really *are* brothers, why do they have to remind us all the time?"

As has been alluded to, children are learning important political lessons from parents and grandparents that directly contradict those ubiquitous rhetorical slogans. Twelve-year-old Silke expressed quite vividly one of the ways in which her dislike and distrust for the Soviet Union was encouraged:

> Whenever my grandmother and I would walk down the street and see a Russian soldier, we would hold hands and squeeze each other's fingers.

That was our signal that we hate the Russians, and it was just between her and me. It was her idea, and now it's our secret. Sometimes she would tell me how bad the Russians were after the war. In school they say they liberated us; but my grandmother says they treated Germans really badly. And now they just tell us what to do. My grandmother says we're not our own country. I don't know about that; but I do wish they would let us travel more.

Occasionally children are even encouraged in the school to hold those same anti-Soviet sentiments. Several children told me of specific teachers of Russian who would give them passing grades in that subject for doing nothing. It was implicitly understood that they need not learn the language of the "oppressor." Unfortunately, such an expression of solidarity often put children in jeopardy; it is very important that they pass their Russian exams when they are older, as the nature of their future educational and employment possibilities depends on this.

Of course, not all children turn on the Soviet Union with resentment or bitterness; there were some with whom I spoke who expressed feelings of affinity for that nation, though such children were in the minority. Twelve-year-old Anna said: "I think that the Soviet Union is pretty good; I have a pen pal in Russia. They always tell us in the school that the Soviet Union is our friend, and I think it might be so. I know in the West they say that the Soviet Union will start another war. But I don't think so. I think the Russians and Berlin understand each other; and I don't think they want a war." Whatever their feelings, the Soviet Union looms large in the minds of these children, just as it does, in reality, on the political horizon of all the Eastern Bloc countries. Yet for those children who direct their anger at the Soviet Union there may be a psychological benefit. Just as West Berlin youngsters have a difficult time holding their nation accountable for events (the war) of which they are ashamed, so do many East Berlin children have difficulty feeling that their nation is in some respects "out to get" them and unresponsive to their needs. Perhaps they feel some relief at being able to locate the "heart of darkness" elsewhere: in this case, in the Soviet Union.

East Berlin children's feelings toward the West are as mixed as are their views of their own nation. It is when they are asked to consider the relative merits of East and West that they begin to give clear expression to their ambivalence. On the one hand, their knowledge that family ties serve to connect the two German states, along with the various favorable images of the West presented on west television, encourages a genuinely positive regard for the West. On the other hand, these children are raised with a very detailed "Feindbild" of the West, which includes West Germany along with the United States and other western powers. It would be wrong to assume that this does not have an effect on children, and in some respects it is buttressed by the negative images of western life that children witness on those same television sets.

Materially, the West often appears as a glittery paradise of sorts, where immediate gratification of desires seems possible. Frequently children would compare their city with the West along material lines—always to the disadvantage of the East. Twelve-year-old Silke detailed her idea of significant differences between East and West Berlin in a drawing (figure 6) that featured the names of the stores to be found in both cities. The first thing she drew was a large, thick border in the center of her paper. The center line is labeled "barbed wire," and it is flanked on either side by thicker bands labeled "mine field"—indeed a threatening demarcation line between East and West. Having effectively divided her page thus, Silke quickly went on to demonstrate her familiarity with West Berlin stores, writing their names hurriedly and with assurance. She then stopped for several minutes, quite unsure as to how she might fill in the East Berlin side of her paper. She insisted that she could think of nothing, and this realization caused her some confusion. Only with the help of several friends who were playing in a nearby room did she finally, with evident dissatisfaction, complete her "picture." About her drawing and the difficulties she encountered, Silke said, "There are so many beautiful things 'over there.' I wish I could visit, just for a day, so I could go to Karstadt or Quelle, and buy things we can't buy here and not have to pay for it! They are so lucky over there. Here, we have nothing like that. Yes, we do have 'nice' shops— Intershop or Exquisitladen—but you either need west money or a *lot* of our money. And I don't have either."

Generally, when asked about the West, children would initially refer to the material advantages, as did Silke. And sometimes children actively seek closer proximity to these same advantages. Several twelve- and thirteen-year-old boys whom I knew frequently hung out at the Bahnhof Friedrichstrasse, one of the major checkpoints between East and West Berlin. Here they would try to meet incoming westerners in the hopes not only of establishing contact with someone from "over there," but also of somehow getting western currency (unlikely) or, at the least, eastern currency of visitors returning to the West. (East currency cannot be taken out of the East.) Twelve-year-old Stephan describes one such occasion that left him a bit of a celebrity in his neighborhood:

A few months ago I came down here with two of my friends. We come here a lot, sometimes just to see people from "over there"—they can be so strange sometimes. Well, this time we met an old "Rentner" [pensioner] from West Berlin, and he started talking to us, showing us his pictures of his family. He was pretty nice. But while we were talking, he found out that he didn't have his camera. And he had pictures of his relatives still in it. He got really upset and ran back to the station. I went with him; he was so old, I thought he would have a heart attack like my grandfather.

We told a guard about it, but no one found the camera. But half an hour later, while we were still looking, they called him over the intercom. Someone found his camera on the S-Bahn and turned it in. That's one good thing about over here, right? "Over there" I don't think anyone would return it. They'd probably just keep it.

Anyway, this man was so happy that he gave me all his leftover east money—about twenty marks. I kept hoping he would give me west money, but I knew he probably wouldn't. When I got home, everyone thought it was great, and I took all my friends out for ice cream. I still go down to the station a lot, but I haven't been lucky since then.

Children are drawn to the West for what it offers. Clearly one of the initial attractions my presence had for children was the implicit promise of "access" to the West: maybe I would be able to bring over various coveted goods from West Berlin. In their desire to get somehow closer to the West, young people will frequent various places in their city that attract westerners: the checkpoints, Alexanderplatz, the Museum Island. Sometimes they come away from such encounters feeling a certain pride in their own nation (as Stephan did when he spoke of the honesty of people in his country), and at other times they learn lessons that contradict their school lessons (as in Stephan's warm, fruitful encounter with a so-called "enemy" of the state).

Yet along with the material wealth in the West comes an attitude that many of children find infuriating. That twelve-year-old boy quoted in chapter 1 said it best: "Sometimes you see these people come over from West Berlin, and they have their BMW, or their nice clothes, and they look at us like they feel sorry for us. And I think maybe they should feel sorry for themselves." Another twelve-year-old said: "I hate some of those people from the West; they are so snotty. They come here with their money and act so big and like they're better than us. Just because they're richer." Many children can end up feeling bitter toward the West because of the way it makes them and their society look in comparison. Such overt expressions of pity from westerners often remind children of their own feelings of inferiority vis-à-vis the West.

And when they are feeling less taken with the glitter and promises of the West, these children are capable of criticizing that place on moral grounds. Occasionally this critique takes on the ring of rhetoric, and children bandy about terms like *socialist* and *capitalist* with ease. Yet for many, these are not just empty words but terms that have acquired a definite meaning and a place in their vocabulary. They are words that deal with the very issues of fairness and equity that children address over and over:

> I think it's bad that there are so many poor people 'over there.' I don't know why there are, especially since there is so much money in the West. But we always hear about the poor and the unemployed—and I think that's true; I can see it on television. Maybe it's that way because it's capitalistic, like we learn here. Whatever it is, it is better here because we are socialist and can get jobs, and there isn't anybody here who has no food and is starving.

Although these children witness the great wealth of western life, they are also witnesses to the poverty there—a reality that is rarely doubted, inasmuch as both east and west television offer glimpses of it, along with the other harsh realities of life under capitalism. Even children who comment on the disparities in wealth and privilege in their own system will often defend that system in comparison to the West: "At least there are no starving people here." I do not feel this sort of comparison is simply a reflection of children's responsiveness to "reality" (it is that, too); many also seem to feel a need to find and assert various advantages to living where they do. It is impossible living in a city that looks worse than its neighbor in every respect.

In addition to appearing excessively preoccupied with money and all too unconcerned about the plight of the poor and unemployed, the West is also frequently perceived as too chaotic. One young girl told me: "Over there you have lots of freedom, but lots of unemployment, too. What good is freedom when you can't find a job? Here we can always find work, even if we don't have freedom like you. And here is not so *hectic* as West Berlin. Over there you always have demonstrations—those people seem crazy sometimes!" The following conversation between two children addresses this and other issues relevant to these East Berlin youngsters.

Sebastian: In America there is a lot of violence and demonstrating, isn't there? More than in West Berlin even, and that's a lot. At least it seems that way on television.

Heiner: No, it's about the same.

S: Well, maybe so. But it's not like that here. Here you have to apply in advance to get permission to demonstrate. And then the demonstrations are peaceful. Still, if I could travel where I want, I'd go to America. I have an uncle who lives in Texas.

H: If I could go to the West, the first thing I'd do would be to visit my aunt in Cologne. She sometimes comes to visit us, and I like her a lot. But then I'd go to America. I'd love to go to one of the oceans and go diving. Or go wind surfing. But we have to stay here. That's why I don't like Honecker. He won't let us travel where we want. He's afraid we'll stay. But I wouldn't; I just want to look around.

S: Well, I'm still not sure that I wouldn't stay in America or "over there." I think about it, and I'm just not sure.

Me: Well, why is the Wall there, and so well defended?

S: The soldiers are there to protect our country—

H: —and to kill people.

S: Yeah, people who want to go to the West. . . . I think they want to leave because of the advertisements from the West. They see those ads and want to go over.

H: Well, then, why don't they just have more advertisements here, so people would want to stay here?

S: It's not just that. Sometimes people from the West try and get over the Wall to us, so they can kill the border soldiers, and take pictures—spies.

At that point both boys chimed in to sing "The Border Soldier Song," with a mixture of seriousness and silliness that made it difficult to be certain as to their feelings behind the song. It seemed, though, that their tone of voice, in singing that song, betrayed the ambivalence they'd just demonstrated with their words.

Twelve-year-old Tanya was quite clear in expressing the advantages she perceived in life in the East.

> The Wall was built because people in the West were taking away our doctors and other skilled people. And we were losing a lot of them that way. Also, they were always going by the border, acting like they were getting ready for a war against us. They didn't want us to live here or something. So the Wall was built. I think we do need the Wall still. When I see the news about the West, all I see is crime, demonstrations, murders—nothing else. Sometimes I think the Wall protects us from all that. Soldiers have died defending the border, you know. We learned about one of them in school. I think it's better here because it's stricter. There are more laws, so we don't have demonstrations like they do in the West. We need those laws; and sometimes I wonder why its not more strict in the West.

There is much truth to Tanya's account: thousands of people were fleeing to the West before the border was sealed. Yet some children appeared to have a greater need to see more of the "bad" side to the West; certainly Tanya was exposed to the positive and negative aspects of the West on television, yet as far as she was concerned, all she sees of it on television is "crime, demonstrations, and murders." However, even Tanya's views are frequently undermined by stories that she hears from her grandmother. "My grandmother tells me a lot about what it was like before they built the Wall. She had all her friends in West Berlin, and she worked over there. One day she came home and noticed there were more soldiers at the border, and the next day the Wall was being built; and she was separated from all her friends. It's so sad; sometimes she cries when she tells me. Then I don't know what to think." As is so often the case, family stories serve to complicate, if not contradict, the clean sweep of rhetoric. One wonders what it will be like for the next generation, growing up in a world without adults who have experienced life before the Wall.

Another way children had of expressing their views on the Wall and the differences between "over there" and their home was to draw. One young girl, Andrea (twelve), often had difficulty finding the right words for her thoughts and feelings, so instead she provided a remarkable drawing that is rich in political and emotional detail (figure 7). Unlike many children her age, who use the weather to differentiate East and West, Andrea has the sun shining on both sides. Before one stops to notice particular details, one observes the striking use of color: four colors used in her depiction of East

Berlin (and somber ones at that), as opposed to eight used for West Berlin. In East Berlin, people with indistinct features wear drab, brown clothes; many of them are lined up outside a sneaker store, while others, dressed in black, are also in line, outside an ice cream café. To the left, near the Wall, is a tiny black car—significantly smaller than the West Berlin auto. At the center of her depiction of the East is a factory, belching smoke from its chimneys—a sign of productivity. Overhead is a symbol of travel limitations imposed on GDR residents: a train heading in the direction of the Soviet Union, Czechoslovakia, Poland, and Hungary, with the GDR at the caboose. This is in dramatic contrast to the image in the West of an airplane traversing the globe—a symbol of freedom to travel anywhere.

In Andrea's portrayal of the West there are no waiting lines. In fact, the picture shows only one person in the West, but that young girl is given distinct features. Andrea seems to suggest that in the West the individual *counts* (sometimes too much), and here one is free from the constant crowds and lines of the East. The girl in her picture is dressed in colorful clothing. Behind her is a large, bright automobile, while in front of her is a small, colorful garden. Music appears to be blaring from the discotheque, and the sneaker store is free of lines. Meanwhile, a factory, much smaller than the one in the East, stands idle, its doors barred—a symbol of widespread unemployment in the West.

Finally, there is the Wall itself; tall and solid, it effectively divides East and West Berlin. Although the border guard carries a black gun, his face remains bland and expressionless, and it is not clear to what degree he is perceived as a threat, or a protector. One of her friends, looking on, exclaimed, "Why are you making the Wall so pretty?" Perhaps Andrea, like many of her peers, is not entirely sure. But this young girl has managed in one sitting to draw a succinct and suggestive portrait of two cities, clearly expressing their significant differences, while with her use of color managing to portray her own sympathies, which definitely appear to lean to the more colorful West—marred mainly, and significantly, by the specter of unemployment.

Regardless of their conflicting views of the two cities that stare implacably at one another across the Berlin Wall, many of these East Berlin children echo Klaus's sentiments; they are seeking something in which to invest their faith and idealism. Some children find that in the political agenda of the GDR. They are able to get involved in the efforts of various youth organizations to send relief to their poor "comrades" in such far-off places as Kampuchea, or as near as Poland. One twelve-year-old girl,

Manuela, who has lived for one year in West Berlin (having spent her earlier years in East Berlin), made the following statement: "One thing I hate about here is that everyone sings Baby Quatch [baby junk]—Cat Stevens and other stuff like that. It's always so stupid; how can they stand it? Over there in the East we sang partisan songs . . . 'I carry a flag / and this flag is red. . . .' Those songs matter!" For children such as her there is a feeling of purpose in the GDR, a feeling that certain ideals *matter*.

Yet many children do not seem able to detect in the various political organs of their nation a chord responsive to their idealistic yearnings. There does not seem to be a lot about their nation that these children can unequivocally love and look up to. And their keepers of history have given them mixed signals: what happened before the war was tainted by capitalism and fascism and therefore should not be associated with the current East German state, *but* there were events and people from that period in which East Germans can still be proud. Yet the interpretation of those people and events varies according to the nation's shifting political climate; and even the government has acknowledged the problem it faces as a nation with too few deeply rooted symbols of its existence and ideals.[6]

At this point all that appears to distinguish the GDR from its eastern neighbors is its relatively higher standard of living. Children and adults alike are proud of and want to preserve this distinction. Yet this pride has to do with being German, not necessarily East German. What children often hear from parents is that because they are German—hardworking, industrious, clever—they have managed to make the most out of a difficult situation. But this is pride in nationality that transcends ideological divisions. And in viewing themselves as Germans (they are taught, by the way, to see themselves as citizens of the German Democratic Republic, not as "plain" Germans), some children then look to the West with a sort of pride and feel a bit like the poor relations: *that* is the part of Germany that has done so well, that has accomplished so much. This feeling of pride in the "other side" gets demonstrated in various ways. One thirteen-year-old boy said this:

> I know a lot about the FRG from television. And I have a lot of relatives over there; and some of them come over to visit us each year. I wish I lived in West Germany; I think I like it better there than here. We should be able to go over if we want to. We're all Germans. But we can't, I know. I'll probably never be able to live over there. Sometimes when I feel bad about my country, I think "at least there's West Germany."

Sometimes I feel like I'm part of both of them—East and West Germany. And that's good; I like what they do in West Germany. I even know more of the politicians there than I do here.

Politically he is a citizen of the German Democratic Republic. Yet by virtue of family he is, as he says, a member of both Germanys. The aspects of West Germany in which these young people feel a measure of pride vary considerably—from the purely political to the world of sports. Something that excited most East German boys (and occasionally girls) like nothing else was a good soccer match; and if the teams playing happened to be West Germany and Spain, these boys rooted for the West German team as though it were their own.

Finally there is the Lutheran church. I would be betraying my experience in East Berlin if I did not at some point say that, despite serious political problems, there is something quite special going on in East Germany. This is especially striking when one travels repeatedly from West Berlin to East Berlin, as has been commented on by other travelers as well. There is a neighborliness between people and a generosity of spirit that is not so evident in the West. East Germans who have fled to the West have remarked on this; they miss the "Rühe" (calm) of East German life, the ways in which people often stick up for one another. Both of the children with whom I spoke who had emigrated from East Berlin to West Berlin said that this was one of the striking differences for them between the two cities. Again, here is Manuela: "Kids over in the East stay together more than here. Here, everyone is for himself—kids fight a lot, or they spend a lot of time alone. I remember one time in school, when I lived 'over there'; one of the kids cracked the world globe and the teacher saw it and wanted to know who did it. All of us kids stuck together, and that teacher never found out. I don't think that would happen here." Perhaps it is the emphasis on concern for the welfare of others that is implied in socialist rhetoric; or it is the community that gets formed in response to oppression. In any case this feeling of community and of mutual responsibility is preserved and nurtured in the church—without all the trappings of the rhetoric which may have contributed to its development.

Unlike the Catholic church in Poland, the Lutheran church is not so clearly linked with nationalism in the GDR; rather, it has become a haven of sorts for individuals frustrated by the saturation of their daily lives with political instruction. One pastor with whom I spoke described the church's role in this way: "Communism today has to do with career advancement.

Individuals do not join the Party because they share the goals and ideals of socialism or communism, but because party membership is essential to getting ahead. The church is beginning to stand for and fight for that which communism used to fight for. Although the state favors the 'begeistert' [committed, enthusiastic] party member, most people trust a church person more than a party person."

The relationship between the church and state has never been close, although relations fluctuate between "warmer" and cold. During my stay in Berlin, Poland's military government had imposed martial law on that nation, and in response the GDR became much more sensitive to opposition within its own ranks. It was at that time that the small GDR peace movement, centered in the church, began gaining momentum—causing a definite strain in church-state relations. In a country that is presumably peaceful, the state feels it cannot allow peace demonstrations which might suggest otherwise.

When the church arrived at a watchword for its peace initiatives—"Swords into ploughshares"—the state forbade the public use of that motto. Instead, it was suggested that young people adopt a slogan aimed more directly at NATO armament plans, and the state produced anti-NATO buttons for those young people to wear. That was a failure, however, as one young woman explained: "Kids won't wear the government buttons because they don't feel they are *theirs;* also, they're ashamed to wear them because the teacher wears them as well." Yet when they choose to wear the buttons of their choice, they inevitably run into trouble:

> Here the state says it is for peace; yet as soon as we wear badges or carry banners showing our support for peace, we're told to break up, leave, go home. Several weeks ago a group of us held our own "demonstration"— really very small, actually. We were wearing peace badges and buttons, and very soon the police came and tore them up and took them away. Then if you go to the chief of police to complain, he acts like he knows nothing about it.—Fifteen-year-old girl

Another minister with whom I became acquainted, Herr Müller (see case study), spoke of the church's role in the peace movement as follows:

> When people here join a peace movement with the church, it's not really with a goal in mind, but usually to have a chance to let out frustrations. We know that we can't reach the goal of a demilitarized society, the way they in the West can imagine. So we are content to at least stay on the

path. For us in the church, a peace movement means we must live with that peace inside of us. *We* must be peaceful, if we are to advocate peace. The peace movement here is so frightening to the government, not because it really is a threat, but because it has not been organized by those on high. It is something out of their control, and that is very scary in a state such as ours. We will stand by our desire to use the biblical say-ing "Swords into ploughshares" as our motto, although the state has forbidden it. You see, it's embarrassing to them, since this is also a sym-bol used by the Soviet Union, our "best friends."

Aside from the blatant political activity it encourages (though church offi-cials insist on the legitimacy of the state and say they will not be identified as "opposition in Christian clothing"), the church also seeks to carry out its traditional mission, encouraging and responding to the need of its mem-bers for religious, not just political nourishment. Herr Müller explains: "We are trying to listen more to our insides, our hearts, and so we pay increasing attention to orthodox liturgy—songs, candles. . . . You see, we Germans are very rational; that is our strength and our weakness. We must now begin to listen more to our feelings."

Many young people become church members not out of well-defined religious motives, or because they necessarily want to become involved in the peace movement. Rather they seek a place that encourages personal expression and shuns political rhetoric. Many of them argue that it is only in the church that they feel like individuals, as though they matter. One thirteen-year-old girl offered this: "I come to my church group and I can finally relax. I say what I feel; I talk about what happened in school. And I know I'm safe here. Other people here have different opinions from mine, but that's not a problem. Nobody is going to turn me in for saying what *I* feel; and this is the only place that I don't have to worry about the state."

Basically, the church offers individuals the chance to be themselves and to speak freely from their hearts, while being members of a larger commu-nity. Thus it provides people an alternative to sinking into apathy and isolated bitterness. Whereas the state encourages (no, insists on) a sense of community, it persistently ignores or punishes the needs and concerns of the individual. The church, on the other hand, offers individuality within community, and it is for that reason that its enrollment is growing at such a rapid pace. As well, the church allows young people to find a way for them-selves that in some respects wends its way between East and West. One young girl told me: "Here we are always told to think of the state's needs.

Always the state! And we begin to forget what other *people* need. I don't think it's better in the West, either—where everyone speaks of 'selbstverwirklichung' [self-actualization]. Always 'me, me' over there. Here in the church we see that we must trust in God, and also that we are responsible for other people, not just for ourselves."

Clearly, children's loyalties are divided in this eastern half of a divided nation. Some turn from their confusion that arises in the face of the contradictory messages they confront daily, and become apathetic, bitter, isolated. Others find some aspect of their nation in which they can invest some trust, from which they can derive some pleasure. Still others turn to the unique consolation offered by the church, or family; or they look to the West for that consolation. They do see themselves as East Germans, but the emphasis for many of them is on the second word, *German*. Like many of their peers in West Berlin, these children are caught between the fixed boundaries of ideology and the more inclusive embrace of a shared German culture, history, and language. They, too, draw on the elements of their experience in an effort to fix themselves in a specific moral and political universe.

Case Study: Torsten

I have an uncle who lives in San Francisco, and he sent me a card a few weeks ago; it's really beautiful there. I think I'd like to visit America— but just to look around, not to stay. Because America is a capitalist country, which means some people are rich and own all the factories, and a lot of people are poor. That's no good. But America has it good in one way. The good thing is they put their weapons over here, so when any of them go off, there's a war here and not in America. I don't want to speak badly of your country, but socialism is better, because here you don't have to worry about war so much. Here it is more peaceful. . . . Well, our country does arm itself too . . . but that's because America does. We *have* to protect ourselves from America, and the FRG.

This was one of the first extended statements made to me by eleven-year-old Torsten, for whom America is a nation that is appealing in its beauty, yet threatening on account of its military strength and presumably aggressive policies. Torsten's assessment resembles that of many of his peers, though as I came to know him better, he felt freer to express his doubts and confusion. He has learned to play it safe, and he has more reason to do so (and a more difficult time doing so) than do many children his age.

Unlike many children whom I met through chance encounters on the back streets of East Berlin, Torsten comes from a family that is well known to the authorities. His father, Sebastian Müller, is a highly respected minister of the Lutheran church and an active participant in the fast-growing East German peace movement. As his church receives financial (and moral) support from its West German brethren, links between both nations are especially strong at the church level, and Herr Müller receives regular visits from his colleagues in the West. In addition, he has been permitted on several occasions to visit certain western European countries on church-related business. Because of the politically delicate nature of his work, it is especially important that Herr Müller and his family maintain as "respectable" a profile as possible. Yet it was the minister, in the face of his wife's serious reservations, who introduced me to his son Torsten, as well as to the rest of the family.

They live in the once fashionable district of Pankow, in the northeast perimeter of East Berlin. The family of five occupies a large apartment, which with five rooms is a luxury in this nation where living space is at an absolute premium. Across the street stand the remains of a church destroyed during the last war; like so many ruins in East Berlin, they are deliberately left standing as a continuing reminder of that war and its fascist origins. Two blocks farther on is a large square, where numerous shops line the street. Although time and the shifting economic priorities of a young socialist economy have contributed to the erosion of the once lovely facades of apartment houses and villas, and the neighborhood is decidedly more heterogeneous than in its prewar days, this area of Pankow still remains one of the more "elite" districts of East Berlin—home of doctors, lawyers, and bureaucrats.

The day that I met Torsten he was sitting on the floor of his bedroom with two of his classmates, surrounded by various maps of East Berlin. They were in the midst of fulfilling a school assignment: to draw up a single map of their city on which the locations of the numerous "Sporthallen" (athletic centers) and associated bus, subway, and streetcar routes were clearly designated. Such assignments are intended not only to familiarize children with their home city but to impress upon them the lengths to which their government goes to take care of its young people. New athletic centers are widely publicized, and indeed some of them are wonderfully equipped (if overcrowded and difficult to reach for many children). Thus the boys' map illustrated the heavy emphasis placed on sport—and the young—in this society. In addition, such assignments teach children to work together in a spirit of cooperation, and the harmony of this particular little group was striking.

Upon entering this scene I was quietly greeted by all three boys, who then returned to their work, interrupted by occasional horseplay. Now and then they made efforts to include me in their banter, but for the most part they were discreet and kept their curiosity well contained. According to Herr Müller, this was the first time any of them had met an American, so their reserved manner was puzzling to me. Months later, Torsten tried to explain his reaction to our first meeting. "I didn't know what to think when my father brought you in. I knew you weren't bad, because my father said it was all right to be with you. But still I wasn't sure how to act. I knew I couldn't tell my teachers I met you, or even a lot of the kids at school. We're not supposed to like Americans."

The occasion of our first meeting brought to the surface a significant conflict for Torsten: his father's word versus that of his teachers in school. Although most of the children I came to know had picked up unorthodox views from one or another family member, few had parents who were so willing to assert their views publicly. This put Torsten in an awkward position: his father's views are well known, yet his son is not really safe to publicly entertain those same views; nor is he altogether sure of their "correctness." Like many children his age, Torsten feels caught between the values of the state (and wanting to please and be recognized by his teachers), and the lessons of his experience, which includes the oft-voiced beliefs of his father and other members of his church.

Occasionally the nature of his father's work and personal convictions causes trouble for Torsten, of which he is well aware:

> I know the church isn't very popular here in the GDR. Not with the teachers, at least. So I don't talk about what my father does, and I just do my work, and act like my friends. But sometimes it's a problem. I had a good friend, Ulrich; and his mother told him he couldn't play with me anymore. She read something Vati said, and decided she didn't want Ulrich to be around me anymore. I still see him sometimes, but he can't stay over at my house, and I can't go visit him.

Although his father's employment has made aspects of Torsten's life difficult, this has not served to drive the boy further into the arms of his teachers. Rather, Torsten appears to identify strongly with his father, and occasionally his words can sound as morally persuasive as those of Herr Müller. At such moments Torsten abandons the rhetoric to which he frequently clings in the face of the uncertainties aroused by my questions, or by my very presence (a friendly "enemy of the state"?). He then moves from the sweeping categorical statements about the nature of capitalism and socialism to a more reflective tone.

> Here the GDR is socialist, so to speak. Well, there are people who say it's not really a socialist country, the way it's supposed to be. I'm not sure who they are. But they say "socialist" means people live peacefully together and try to be peaceful with other nations as well. But here we do have weapons. And there are all these signs telling us we must fight with the Soviet Union to defend peace; and in school they say we must hate West German soldiers, and that we will have to fight them in a war. And then they say we are defending peace. How can we defend peace with guns?

When Torsten says he "does not know who" these people are, he is not being altogether candid, and his words betray his desire to "protect" his father by cloaking him in anonymity. For it is just people like Herr Müller and members of his parish who voice such sentiments.

Of course, the Wall, when seen as a means of preventing escape, is the ultimate contradiction confronting Torsten and other children. Quite familiar with its existence, Torsten nonetheless always had difficulty speaking of it. The first few times I would broach the subject, he would provide me with a detailed account of the reasons for the building of the Wall that was virtually identical to the accounts given in his textbooks. It was as though this was one topic he simply could not risk discussing. Later he would give me a look of impatience and remind me that we had "already talked about that."

Yet, some time after we had gotten to know one another, Torsten decided to draw me a picture of that Wall (figure 8). The act of creating seemed to help him tap into his deeper convictions, bypassing official statements that frequently lie at the forefront of his (and most children's) consciousness. In his picture a West German soldier stands to one side of the Wall in full combat gear. Nearby flies his nation's flag, and over them both droops a leafless tree. The Wall itself is portrayed in detail, with the barbed wire on the eastern side. It is an effective barrier between East and West. On its other side a tank aims its guns at the West. Overhead hangs a sad sun. "It's not really well drawn, but I think it gets a lot across," Torsten explained. "The sun is unhappy as it looks down on the border; the tree is bare, because that's what happens to trees on the border, or during a war. See, he's defending his side from the other side, and the other side is doing the same thing." When asked where he might be in this drawing, Torsten made an effort to distance himself from this picture of grim reality: "I'm far away in the background. You can't see me. They want to defend peace, they say here. But they do it with weapons. I think a gun from here is the same as a gun from over there. It doesn't matter which side shoots first, because both will shoot. And then where is peace? The only way to really defend peace is with yourself. Show you are peaceful without guns. I don't care who is capitalist and who is socialist. The main thing is that there is no more war."

What is immediately evident about his drawing is Torsten's obvious familiarity with things military. In this respect he is very much like his peers, most of whom are quite adept at portraying accurately military vehicles and uniforms. It is also interesting that Torsten placed the sad sun directly over the East Berlin tank. Is it *more* sad in the East? Also, he used an impersonal object as a symbol of his nation's aggression; I am reminded of Andrea's drawing, where the people in East Berlin were left anonymous, the "faceless crowd." The East German state does not often single out politicians for recognition; rather, children hear incessantly of the Party or of the state, and they are "the people" (das Volk). Yet in the West, Torsten places a human being and a tree—signs of life and individuality, caught up in war. The Wall is a depressing and deathly place, a nodal point of tension and aggression. As he discussed his picture, Torsten sounded very much like his father—especially in his insistence that we carry peace within ourselves and demonstrate it in the ways we act toward one another. Over time I realized that the issue of aggression—how to manage it—was central to Torsten, as it is to many children.

Yet not all children in East Berlin would subscribe to Torsten's brand of pacifism. Certainly not all children come from families where questions of right and wrong, good and evil are the foundation of their fathers' or mothers' professional lives. In such a home environment Torsten has had to deal with his own aggressive feelings in a particular fashion; he is, for the most part, very well behaved and is even solicitous toward his younger brother, who could frequently be quite provocative. Although Torsten has pushed his aggression to the side, by a number of psychological defense maneuvers, it is still of central importance to him—as it is for his father, who wages his own struggle with aggression on a personal and a political level.

The only time I was witness to Torsten's anger was when we engaged in puppet play. Here, he felt free to yell and hit various puppet characters, though the one character for whom he reserved the brunt of his anger was a policeman puppet. Sometimes he would provide "reasons" for his anger: "We call them our 'Grüne'; they're green on the outside and empty on the inside. They're always trying to get you for something. Especially on the highway when you're going for a trip. They even put branches and leaves on their cars and wait on the other side of the road to trap you for speeding or something." Now, this is perfectly likely; many of East Berlin's young people learn early to distrust and dislike the police, and feel free to say so. Yet I suspect that what makes that anger especially potent for Torsten is that it gets linked up with his particular struggles with parental authority, as he tries to assert himself in the face of various familial rules and restrictions. Yet with the desire to break free from externally imposed limitations on personal freedom comes the fear of having *no* control. When Torsten expresses worries about a society that may not be able to prevent an outbreak of aggression within or without its boundaries, he is certainly speaking of a real and significant political concern, and he is perhaps also demonstrating concern over his own capacity to do likewise. Here that elusive connection between the political and psychological becomes somewhat clearer.

In his struggles with authority Torsten is contending particularly with his father, toward whom he has a mixture of feelings, as does any child toward a parent. Yet this struggle is complicated by the fact of Herr Müller's frequent absences from home. He is a very busy man, and his work sometimes takes him far afield—to the West and the other side of the Wall. This is not always easy for Torsten; and at one point he said to his father: "Vati, I still remember my seventh birthday when you were in Holland. I was sad you couldn't be here, but you sent me such a nice card. It's my favorite in my collection now." That may all be true, yet it is difficult for Torsten to openly express the anger he may also feel. Were he to do so, he would risk losing the few times he does share with his father; in addition, suppression of anger is a valued trait in the Müller family (unless it is expressed in the political manner of Herr Müller).

These trips of Herr Müller's prompt Torsten to speculation about the West. And although they make the minister unavailable to his son, they also have their advantages. In speaking of his father's trips Torsten says:

I don't see my father very much; he makes a lot of business trips. Sometimes he goes to places in the GDR; and other times he goes to other countries. He's been to England and Holland and West Berlin. I wish I could go with him; but I can't. It's forbidden. Children can only go to Hungary or Czechoslovakia. I don't even think adults can go to the West either—unless they go on business like Vati. The only ones who can go are pensioners. And we can't go because the West is capitalist and we are socialist.

Torsten talks about his father's trips with a measure of pride and envy. That his father does visit the West is a distinction of sorts—one that sets Torsten apart from his friends. On his return from such trips Herr Müller is always sure to bring toys and games back with him—much to Torsten's delight. His bedroom might be confused for that of any of his West Berlin peers, and this certainly does not hurt Torsten's popularity among his friends. His father's special occupation is a mixed blessing, as he knows.

Yet when he is asked directly about the differences between East and West, Torsten frequently mouths official rhetoric; it is only indirectly, or through direct observation, that his ambiguous feelings become evident. Often he will veer between the one and the other in the course of a single conversation—testing the waters, so to speak.

> The Wall is there to keep out spies from the West, who want to hurt us. There are people in the FRG and in West Berlin who don't like the GDR at all, so they say it just isn't there at all. And shouldn't be. I think they think we're always building weapons; but it's America that is militaristic. But I don't think it's all bad over there; I'd like to visit just to look around, not to live there. There people can travel where they want to; the police aren't always around, making sure you do what you're supposed to. And also, people over there are German, too. I have another uncle who lives in Frankfurt in the FRG. They are stopping me from seeing him, too. I wish they could keep out the bad people from over there and let us go visit.

For children like Torsten the West is an enemy, intent on undermining the autonomy of his nations. Yet the West is also the home for other Germans, and as such cannot be just an enemy. It is indeed difficult to sort out. And a child like Torsten is being pulled in two directions: by the state (the school) and by the church and his family.

Torsten is a member of a Pioneer group and is somewhat proud of that. He was eager to show me his membership card, complete with passport photo, rules for how a proper Pioneer conducts himself, a brief life of Ernst Thälmann (for whom the organization is named), as well as a history of the GDR. Although Torsten does not have to carry this around at all times, he does bring it to school on days when he has meetings. His membership dues are minimal: ten pfennigs a month (a few pennies). Torsten appears to enjoy his meetings, although he is occasionally cautioned by his parents and his older brother against taking all of his "lessons" too seriously. Yet certain ideas and facts inevitably sink in, as Torsten indicated while we looked over his social studies notebook. "I haven't memorized everything about people like Marx or Rosa Luxemburg; but we have to write so much about them that pretty soon you begin to notice them. It is the same with Lenin, Engels, Liebknecht; sometimes I think I know about them without having to study at all."

At times Torsten would provide me with a history lesson, and on such occasions he would beam and appear proud—both of what he knew and of his country. He, the insider, was initiating me, the outsider, into some of the important aspects of his nation. Sometimes this would be done jestingly, as when he would ask me, out of the blue: "What's the biggest socialist country in the world, Tom?" When I responded, "the Soviet Union," he would laugh and say "Jah!" At other times he would appear more serious, and although such "lessons" were almost direct quotes from a textbook, it seemed to matter to Torsten that I hear him out. Here, for example, is his explanation of communism: "Socialism is the forerunner of communism. Do you want to know what communism is? Well, Lenin said at the time of the October revolution 'out of these fallen shall rise a great "Werkstatte" [factory].' See. Communism makes the dreams of the people come true. You have to imagine what it was like then—everything destroyed after the revolution, and out of the ruins and the swamps the people built up the first socialist country." Such a history does capture the imagination of children like Torsten, for it offers a dramatic picture of suffering, struggle, and finally redemption of sorts.

Yet Torsten is being pressed by the church and his family to consider alternate interpretations of his and his nation's experience. I accompanied him one fall day to a "Kinderfest" put on by one of the neighborhood churches. At the outset of the party, as we all sat in the church pews, we were invited to join in song. We were given a song sheet, at the top of which was written "Only for use within the church!"—a warning of sorts. The first song started out as follows, and was sung with enthusiasm by the thirty or so children present:

Ich möchte gerne Brücken bauen,
wo tiefe Gräben nur zu sehn.
Ich möchte uber Zäune schauen,
um auch den Andern zu verstehen.

(I want to build bridges,
where there are only deep ditches.
I want to look over fences,
to be able to understand the others.)

Treated metaphorically, it can be seen as a song enjoining people to try to understand one another better; yet given the political realities of East Berlin, words like *fence* or *wall* become politicized—especially when one speaks of transcending them!

Here and at home Torsten hears the Christian message of peace and reconciliation, which inevitably becomes a message of political opposition as well. He has a personal investment in that message, by virtue of inclination, perhaps, and certainly because of the intimate nature of the relationship between his family and the church. His participation in the church frequently gives Torsten the support he needs in order to question certain given "truths," without at the same time totally undermining his feelings toward his nation, which are mixed.

> They say we are a peaceful nation, that what we have here is better than in the West. If that is true, why aren't we allowed to visit the West? Why wouldn't we want to return here if it really is better? I don't think we are peaceful here, like they say. We are always learning to hate the Germans "over there"; but I think we must try to find peace with them.
>
> And over there, is not all good either. I think there is more chance to do what you want. But there are too many poor people there. Still, I think we should try to get to know them. We shouldn't be always fighting with each other; we are like a family, even if we are different.
>
> I think it would be a good idea for children here to meet children over there in West Berlin. Adults get stuck fighting with each other and can't seem to stop. But if kids get to know each other, and like each other, then maybe they'll remember that when they grow up and become adults. Then when they're making the decisions, maybe they'll make different decisions than their parents do.

In a sense, Torsten is a peacemaker. Like so many children in East Berlin, he is struggling to find and assert his own beliefs between the various demands and values of the state and those of his family and the church. Each has its peculiar hold on him, and as Torsten knows well, it is impossible to casually dismiss one in favor of the other. His allegiances are complicated, as family loyalties and grievances get tied up with a wide, often confusing range of political and moral concerns. His task is to try to negotiate his way through these complex and often conflicting aspects of his personal and national life.

6 | Conclusion

This has been a study of the manner in which children enlist political and historic reality in their personal struggle to achieve a coherent moral and political vision. For children in East and West Berlin the political situation is indeed complicated. A city that was once the capital of a powerful nation, albeit one with a fragile sense of cohesion and identity, now stands divided by the Berlin Wall—a minor recapitulation of the larger division of the German nation. Although the two cities still remain connected in various important ways, they have come to embody two antagonistic political systems—that of state socialism and western capitalism.

Yet the issue is not just that of two opposing ideologies confronting one another across a national border. Rather, these are two distinct ideologies wedded to *German* people, *German* history, *German* culture, and very importantly, the *German* language. These children, then, are confronted by the fact of their differences (ideologically rooted) as well as the fact of their common heritage. Seen in this light, the current division of Germany, initially perceived as the solution to the "German problem," only highlights the difficulties the nation has faced for centuries. They are difficulties faced by a collection of people sharing a common culture and language and living on a patch of earth with no natural boundaries of its own. Commonly referred to as the "Land der Mitte" (the nation in the middle), this collection of German-speaking people was always under the constant pressure and influence of outsiders, a fact that contributed to the persistent regionalism of the area, thwarting various efforts at unification. In fact, at an earlier time in its history, the territory of Germany was divided by another wall, the Limes Germanicus—built by the Romans through southern and western Germany to separate provinces under their control from those considered barbaric. Although that wall was destroyed long ago, it too left its legacy: a cultural barrier that separated the area in the south influenced by the Church of Rome from the Protestant north.

Today it is not religion but politics that divides the nation. Children in both cities of Berlin—the first generation to grow up with the Berlin Wall—are left to make sense of this striking political predicament. Who are we and what do we believe in? What does our nation stand for? And how are we to regard those people and that nation "over there"? It is the stark presence of the Wall that inevitably frames their questions: what or who does this barrier keep out, or protect us from; and what is included within its bounds? In their efforts to address these questions, children look carefully at their surroundings and listen to what they are taught, often finding themselves somewhere between the demands of rhetoric and the larger embrace of a common culture, history, and language. How do these children persist as Germans, while at the same time becoming something else—socialist or capitalist Germans?

Stepping back from the lives of these young people, one can speak of the importance of language in perpetuating a culture and defining and carrying on its particular values and objects of concern. Walter Abish says, "Basically we remain German because our language permits us to glimpse what our ancestors saw when they climbed a mountain or entered a forest or undertook a difficult journey."[1] Yet German is spoken in other nations—Austria and Switzerland—that do not feel a national kinship with Germany. And there is evidence that the language itself is being systematically altered in the GDR to reflect that nation's ideological priorities.

The emotional charging of words, the excessive use of superlatives, the preference for terms taken from the military vocabulary, the sharp schematization that eliminates neutral valuations in favor of black-white dichotomies, the insistent use of invective, and the constant repetition of stereotyped epithets . . . are in use once more. So, moreover, are words that are also used in the West but have, in the GDR, a profoundly different meaning—words beginning with the prefix "peace," or the adjectives "people's" and "popular," words like "coexistence" and "relaxation of tension" and "human rights" and "democracy."[2]

If a language is at the heart of a culture, then this radical shift in its use may, over time, serve to effectively distance the GDR from the FRG. Already it is obvious to children that linguistic differences matter somehow. One twelve-year-old girl in West Berlin said this of one of her new classmates who was recently permitted to leave the GDR with her family: "I can't really explain it, but she's different from us somehow. You can tell when she talks; she just talks different from us."

Still, these children maintain a powerful feeling of connection to the people "over there." Most of them have family in the other Germany, and this is perhaps the most powerful fact to undermine the divisiveness engendered by rhetoric. In addition, all of these children have parents with memories that include a Berlin before the Wall and grandparents whose memories begin with a unified German nation. And unlike the nations of Switzerland and Austria, these two nations are German. Their names are constant reminders of that fact: East and West *Germany*. Children are aware of this, and it prompts them to address their relationship with the "other" Germany. Twelve-year-old Boris from West Berlin said: "West Berlin belongs to the FRG, and East Berlin belongs to Russia. But the people over there are like us. We were all Germans once—same language, same religion, same ideas. And we all have relatives over there still." And twelve-year-old Helmut in East Berlin had this to say: "If I could, I think I would go over there, at least to visit. We learn that they are our enemy, and I'm just not sure; maybe some of them are. But we have relatives there, and I *know* they're not our enemy. They visit us each year, and I like them a lot. We're the same really; we just live in different places."

One cannot help but wonder what will happen when those personal ties to the past and to the "other side" vanish. When these children grow up and have their own children, what will they pass on? And their children? Will the historical fact of a unified German nation (however brief in the course of European history) become a myth of sorts, perpetuated in stories? Or will it be forgotten? Will the process begun with the division of the nation in 1945 reach its culmination in two distinct nations with different memories tied to different histories and culture? How much *does* the fact of family transcend ideological barriers? Torsten said: "When all your family and friends are somewhere in one country, you want to be there, too. That's how I feel here. I'd like to travel to the West, but this is my home, where my family is. So I want to live here, too." Although he is speaking of family living in the East, there are children who share his sentiments whose families are spread across the two Germanys. In their case it appears that allegiance to a nation is complicated by this keen awareness of a connection that overrides political differences. Certainly this relationship between family and state needs to be more closely regarded.

In light of what I heard in both cities it appears likely that children in the West will lose sight of their connection with the East more readily than their peers "over there" will abandon their association with the West. East Berlin children are more highly motivated to maintain their western connection. Through family relations and, very significantly, through western television programming, these youngsters see the West as holding out the promise not just of a material "paradise," but of various freedoms all too easily abrogated in the East. If the nation "over there" were not German, perhaps these children could more readily disassociate themselves from its attractions, or from some feeling, passed on by parents and grandparents, that it was only by virtue of the accidents of geography and fate ("Schicksal") that they lost the opportunity to enjoy the privileges of life in the "other" Germany.

The GDR has to find something around which its own people can rally, something in which they can invest a measure of pride—a fact of which that nation's leaders are well aware. Perhaps when the GDR accumulates enough of its own history and can refer more confidently to its own unique national experience, then children will more readily identify with it and express less concern about their ties to the West.

The children in West Berlin appear to have less reason for insisting on their ties to East Germany. They recognize the links forged by family, yet otherwise they appear more willing to concede that the GDR is its own nation. At this point in time, when the balance appears to fall in favor of the West—materially and in terms of personal freedoms—there may be no cause to look carefully at the East and insist on a relationship with it. Yet who can say what will happen over time, as these two political systems mature. Will socialism's inherent advantages and possibilities become more fully realized as the built-in inequities of capitalism become more evident? What then? How will children then regard life "over there"?

This is not simply a study of the feelings of relatedness between children in East and West Berlin; I have also tried to document the various ways in which they perceive and use the fact of the Wall and their separateness. At times their observations reflect preoccupations that are important for children on a personal as well as a political level. For one, the complicated relationship between freedom and security is mentioned repeatedly, along with the manner in which either society addresses that relationship. West Berlin youngsters generally criticize the East for its lack of personal freedoms and heavy reliance on repression, yet they also indicate that with repression comes security and another kind of freedom—freedom from the chaos and anxiety these children experience in their own city. And in East Berlin, children long for the freedoms of the West, yet recognize the apparent lack of restraints evident in the street demonstrations and crime of West Berlin. In contrasting the two Berlins in this regard, many young people forge their own ideas as to how an ideal society would manage this particular set of issues.

Political considerations aside, children are quick to voice moral comparisons of East and West Berlin. The near presence of a different moral, let alone political, order prompts them to evaluate the way both nations handle issues of fairness and justice. Children are not so much comparing the realities of life in these two cities as they are comparing the ideals espoused by the political systems they represent. In this regard the East appears to fare somewhat better in their estimation. Children in West Berlin look at their city and cannot help but see the enormous discrepancies in individual wealth; in contrast, socialism appears to diminish those particular inequities. And although children living in East Berlin are in a better position to see the gap between rhetoric and reality in their city, they also suspect that theirs is still a fairer society than is the West.

What distinguishes these children is their degree of familiarity with that nation "over there." Ironically, children in West Berlin, where freedom of information is by and large guaranteed, know very little about the East; whereas children in East Berlin are flooded with information about the West, primarily through television. Without ever leaving their living rooms they are in a position to compare the official rhetoric in which they are immersed with "reality" as it is served up on their television screens. Much more than their peers in West Berlin, these youngsters are decidedly at the center of a continuing ideological struggle between East and West.

These children are also distinguished by their vastly different relationship to their government. In the East there is a little tolerance for ambiguity in public life; the individual learns early what is expected of him and what he is up against. Of course, such a rigidly defined political system can contribute to depression and apathy in young people as they realize just how little latitude there is for expression of disagreement. Yet in knowing clearly who or what they are contending with—be it an official ideological belief system or a specific figure of authority—children may also be in a position to more clearly define what it is they do believe in. They can fix themselves and their beliefs against the quite solid and well-defined ideological structure of their nation. In contrast, children in the West are surrounded with ambiguity—especially in the wildly diverse and tolerant city of West Berlin. They may have a much more difficult time defining themselves and their beliefs in such a laissez-faire atmosphere.

This particular contrast between East and West becomes most apparent when an individual leaves the East for the West. Despite West German recognition of immigrating East Germans as citizens of the FRG, the person making the move from GDR to the FRG frequently suffers from bewilderment and depression, as he is faced not only with the range of material choices in the West but with the apparent range of ideological choice. As one youth told me: "A big problem for me here is the bookstores. In the GDR the problem was that everything was Marx and Lenin—very one-sided. But I knew where I stood. Here I can find anything from books by neo-Nazis to I don't know what. How's a person supposed to decide what's true? I'm not sure anymore *what* I'm supposed to think."

These two antagonistic ideologies also manage to drive a wedge of fear between the children of these two German nations. In East Berlin, children are taught not simply to fear some abstraction called "capitalism" or "the West"; they are encouraged to fear and distrust West German soldiers who, along with the support of the United States, are poised in readiness for battle with the GDR. And in the West, children see the military fortifications along the Wall and learn early of the Soviet threat to their city. This fear of the other is complicated, and not to be dismissed lightly. It is, after all, rooted in reality; two opposing systems do face one another across the Wall, and as such they are enemies, regardless of other ties between them.

And the idea of war and related suffering is not an abstraction either. These are children growing up in two nations where the evidence of the destructive power of war is everywhere—in the bullet-scarred apartment houses still standing in East Berlin and the remains of the Gedächtniskirche at the head of Kurfürstendamm in West Berlin, to the painful memories and stories of the parents and grandparents of these youngsters. The very division of their nation, and the unremitting presence of the Wall dividing the two cities of Berlin, are testimony to the last of those wars. This fear, then, can be exploited in the service of further eroding feelings of relatedness with the other Germany; and one must wonder what children will feel, and fear, in the future, when time alone has significantly weakened those important familial bonds.

Yet that fear, stimulated by the collective memories of past wars, can also serve to mobilize young people in both nations in an effort to reduce current risks of war—this time a nuclear conflagration. There are peace movements in both nations, although the one in the GDR is vigorously persecuted. Their efforts have been directed at circumventing the divisiveness of ideological claims, and some members of those movements speak of needing a unified, demilitarized Germany to stand as a buffer between East and West. Although that is unlikely, the peace movements have engaged the imaginations of young children and often encourage in them a feeling that the fates of the respective Germanys are bound up with one another. One twelve-year-old East Berlin girl told me: "I don't care who's capitalist and who's socialist. That doesn't matter to me, as long as there isn't another war."

As children struggle between an ideological identity and an identity that transcends ideology, they are in constant search of something larger than themselves in which they might believe. And they frequently express bitter disappointment at not being offered something especially worthy of their allegiance. Children in West Berlin see the Wall and are reminded of their nation's past—a past that manages to endure over time, in the city's land-scape and the memories of its elders. For these children the past is very near, and many of them speak with sadness and shame about that period in their national life. It is a moment that has not been forgotten elsewhere in Europe either; so whether they are at home in Berlin or traveling to Spain or Greece, these youngsters are confronted with the consequences of that past. Such a reality makes it difficult for them to express genuine pride in being German; in fact, they frequently describe themselves and their nation in very negative terms.

If they are to muster up any pride at all, it is when they view the life "over there" and are able to say (with evident relief) that they live in the "freer" of the two Germanys. They frequently can turn on the East as a means of minimizing dissatisfaction with their own lot. Of course the East also manages to highlight certain deficiencies of life in the West—especially the raging "Konsumkultur" so evident in West Berlin and elsewhere in the Federal Republic. Pride in their nation's ability to stock its various shops to the point of bursting does not always sustain citizens, especially when they are unable to actively participate in that frantic quest for more and more.

Although children in East Berlin are provided an ideological perspective that allows them to more easily distance themselves from the German past and to see themselves as a new and distinct nation, they nonetheless search for some object of belief as well. For these children the Wall is not so much a reminder of the past; nor is it an inconvenience as it is in the West, or just protection from western aggression. Most of them realize that the Wall was designed to keep them in, and as such it forces them to make an intense effort at national self-scrutiny. What they see is a highly politicized regime that denies them certain freedoms, where the consequences for breaking particular rules of behavior or thought are serious and painful. This is then exacerbated as they contrast their experience with that of their neighbors, who also happen to be German.

Some children react to this by asserting their German identity, thereby allying themselves with the other Germany, which they admire in many respects. This also allows them to disassociate themselves somewhat from their East German identity. Yet in spite of their clear attraction for the various freedoms and glitter of the West, they manage to uphold a sense of the inequities of that system. At the same time they are well aware of the calm and neighborly tone of their lives, in stark contrast to the "Hektik" of the West. Certain values of cooperation and concern for others have developed in the GDR, either encouraged by ideology or arising in reaction to it. These values are further nurtured by the church—an institution that respects the individual while providing a community that upholds these values and beliefs initially honored by socialist idealism and later lost in the machinery of bureaucracy. In a nation such as East Germany this church-state dichotomy has taken on powerful moral (and hence, political) significance. It would be important to further inquire as to how a child's allegiance to the church supports or undermines his feelings of loyalty to the state.

Although children in East and West Berlin use the fact of the Wall in similar ways, they are also learning different lessons in their respective cities—lessons that have to do with power and with what matters morally, economically, and personally. At times they learn what is intended for them, and other times they arrive at observations that, at the least, complicate their development as members of a given ideological system. As children generally are, they are carefully attuned to the world around them, doing their best to organize the mass of information and experience that is the grist for their feelings of national affiliation or alienation. I have tried to give voice to their various considerations, as they look in wonder and no little confusion at the reality of East and West Berlin. These children are indeed taken up with the task of becoming members of their respective nations; they are German *and* they are growing up in two nations that insist that they are different kinds of Germans. Presently these youngsters maintain a sense of themselves as both Germans and as East or West Germans; and the emphasis they place on either of those identities depends on a range of factors: familial, political, moral, and psychological. One is left to ask whether, over time, they will begin to place that emphasis on the prefix to the word *German,* so that they are, ultimately, *East* Germans as opposed to *West* Germans. And will these nations respond to that eventuality (if indeed it is such) by striking the word *German* (a last vestige of their connection) from their respective names? Will the division of a nation, arbitrarily established forty years ago, finally take firm root in the minds of the next generation of children, so that the sense of connection with the other Germany is only a vague trace in a collective memory?

Epilogue | Four Years Later

I returned to East and West Berlin for a brief visit during the summer of 1986, hoping to discern the ways in which the cities had changed and to discover, too, where some of the children were—most of them by now fifteen and sixteen years old. The Pan Am carrier from Frankfurt delivered me to Tegel Airport in West Berlin on the thirteenth of August, the twenty-fifth anniversary of the building of the Berlin Wall. The rhetoric of West Berlin and West German politicians was familiar, as were the news reports on television and in the local press. All spoke with angry eloquence against the cruelty of the Wall and all that it implies. They spoke, too, with a guarded hopefulness—hope that one day the need for a Wall will pass, that the violations of human rights in the German Democratic Republic will cease, and that relations between the two Germanys can to some degree be normalized. There were demonstrations, as well—small by the standards set by the wild street demonstrations of five years ago. Yet they were at moments quite dramatic, as when a group of protesters charged Checkpoint Charlie and tried to do damage to the entryway and to the adjoining Wall.

In East Berlin, of course, the day was prominently feted (at least officially). The Wall is still described as the "antifascist defense barrier," a necessary support to the integrity—political and economic—of the German Democratic Republic. There were the obligatory parades and displays of military strength along Karl Marx Allee, and dutiful onlookers whose faces etched in dull resignation offered a sharp contrast to the vibrant red of the flags they were to carry and wave. In the Museum for German History, along Unter den Linden, there was a major display detailing the history and significance of the Berlin Wall. The exhibit was not heavily attended.

Of course, in cities that are so well versed in the language of rhetoric and outrage, the complex picture of reality sometimes gets lost. And it is that picture which continues to be of such interest. Not long after the "celebrations" in East Berlin a young couple and a child executed a daring escape through Checkpoint Charlie. Driving a van at high speed, they managed to plow through the checkpoint under a hail of bullets and arrive safely in West Berlin. Certainly the news of that escape through the "antifascist defense barrier" was seen on thousands of East Berlin television sets tuned in to west news broadcasting. Remembering Gritt's first media-conveyed experience of an escape attempt, I thought of all the young children who in the same way witnessed the details of this latest escape. What happens when rhetoric is repeatedly assaulted by fact, by personal observation?

And in West Berlin there was the story of the young auto mechanic who, in an effort to escape his own personal demons and pain, rammed his car at high speed into the Wall, resulting in a fiery explosion and his immediate death. It continues to be strange, the uses to which the Wall is put—psychologically and existentially, as well as politically and economically.

If the Berlin Wall appeared the same (except for the fact that it was more wildly painted and scrawled over on the West Berlin side), the two cities had undergone noticeable changes—at least on the surface. The dominant impetus for various cosmetic alterations in both East and West Berlin is the fact that 1987 is the 750th anniversary of the founding of Berlin. It will be interesting to see how two cities with such avowedly different ideological agendas will celebrate a moment that sets their histories in perspective of a common history dating back more than seven hundred years. Some West Berlin officials have hope that the year will be an opportunity for securing closer relations with East Berlin, and to that end they have invited several prominent East Berlin politicians to participate in the events in West Berlin. At the time of my visit a similar invitation from the GDR had not been made. In any case, both cities were busy preparing for the festivities: renovation and building was going on at an unprecedented rate in East and West Berlin as the cities made an effort to put their best faces forward. West Berlin, in addition, is sponsoring an exciting architecture exhibition, which had already yielded several striking apartment complexes, especially in the Kreuzberg district.

In other ways, too, the cities had changed since my first visit. In certain respects West Berlin was a far quieter city, having gotten through the worst of the "Hausbesetzerszene" and the anti-American demonstrations that had preceded the deployment of U.S. missiles on West German soil. By offering the squatters financial incentives and the opportunity to own the dilapidated houses in which they were living, the city quite effectively defused that tension and violence, so that by the summer of 1986 one would hardly know that there had been such turmoil only four or five years earlier.

The tension that does remain is in connection with foreigners living in the city. Although the Berlin senate made provisions for encouraging Turkish guest workers to return to their homeland (they are offered economic incentives to do so), most of them continue to realize that they can do better if they remain in the city. Expressions of "Ausländerhass" (hatred, distrust of foreigners) had increased in response to the steady stream of political and economic refugees heading for West Berlin. Due to the liberal asylum laws of the Federal Republic of Germany, that country has become the destination of refugees from Sri Lanka, several African nations, and elsewhere. West Berlin is particularly inviting in that refugees flying into Schönefeld Airport in East Berlin can simply walk through a checkpoint into West Berlin. Needless to say, this has been a continual source of strained relations between East and West Berlin. During the summer of 1986 the mood in West Berlin was one of impatience and frustration. Tent communities were set up in each of the districts of the city to accommodate the growing numbers of homeless refugees. Document checks were increasingly common on the subway, while the growls of resentment on the part of West Berliners grew louder. I was reminded that West Berlin is in some respects a city of outsiders; it is full of people drawn to economic possibility, yet full of the most painful homesickness and alienation.

It is in this unique environment where high culture, conservative business values, alternative life-styles, East-West political tension, and racial tensions mix that I sought out some of the children I'd known before. Some had moved away; others were still on vacation during my stay. Matthias, who five years earlier had been convinced he would move to Australia at the first opportunity, was now just seventeen and beginning his apprenticeship as a hairdresser in the district of Wedding. He continues to live with his mother and his younger brother and sister. The family now lives directly next to the Wall. Matthias finds it strange that he can look out the kitchen window and see directly into East Berlin. They live so close to the Wall, in fact, that Matthias's mother one day inadvertently caused an "incident." Directly along the Wall runs the S-Bahn (now owned and operated by West Berlin). Prior to the building of the Wall, their street ran under the S-Bahn and on into what is now East Berlin. The bridge remains, though it is now boarded up. Technically, East Berlin territory extends to the very edge of the bridge, where the street begins to pass beneath it. It is an area that appears to be in West Berlin, as it lies on that side of the Wall. One day, in a hurry to get home to her children, Matthias's mother parked her car along the street, leaving the rear bumper extending by half a foot into East German territory. Within an hour her car was surrounded by East German police, West German police, and American and French soldiers. She was not allowed to move the vehicle until the "incident" (as it was called) was cleared up. It is events like this that not only point up the surreal nature of this kind of political arrangement, but also become the fodder for the political and moral imagination of children like Matthias, or his younger brother.

Matthias claims that his interest in such things has diminished; he is now more concerned with finding a good job and "getting on with my life." "The only thing I'd like them to do with the Wall now would be to take it from Berlin and instead put it around the politicians—Reagan, Kohl, Gorbachev. We could call it a zoo, and put up a sign: 'Please don't feed the politicians.' " He goes on:

> It's strange how you change. To tell you the truth, I'm happy to be German now. I know I used to hate it. But I believe now that I am *not* responsible for what happened forty years ago. Other people can say what they will; I am not going to blame myself anymore. I guess you could say I'm not so political now as I was then. What can I do, really? The politicians run the show, and in the meantime I have to work. My dream now is to go to New York, or Paris, and do film and theater makeup. I'd love to be able to work with Michael J. Fox, or some other American film stars.
>
> I don't think the same things bother me now, like they did when you first met me. I just don't worry the way I used to. I know I used to worry about atomic war all the time; that was one of the reasons I wanted to move to Australia. But I don't really feel so frightened now—even though Chernobyl was pretty scary. I guess I feel I could just as easily get killed on the street here in West Berlin. . . . It's not that I don't think about any of these things anymore; it's just that I have other things to think about as well. I wouldn't say I've become more conservative

though; in fact, I hate the government here in Berlin [a conservative coalition]. But it's hard for me to say I'm a 'leftist' either. I listen to some of them preach about health and about radiation and the environment, and then I see them smoking dope. That doesn't make any sense to me. I guess I still have my own ideas, and maybe I'll never be part of a group. That doesn't worry me.

For someone who is "not so political" as he once was, Matthias continues to offer thoughtful appraisals of the world around him. His attitude toward politicians has remained fairly consistent, though his resentment (so apparent five years ago) is now tempered by a degree of indifference, along with the realization that he has no real influence on such people. Of course, his life has changed. Older now, he is faced with career choices and the limitations and possibilities that are part of those choices. His sights are focused, for the time being, on his immediate situation. Still, in a short visit it was difficult to ascertain whether Matthias remains as untroubled as he claims to be by many of the questions that plagued him as a young boy. I suspect that at the age of ten, eleven, twelve, children are open to these issues and capable of feeling them in a heartfelt way, willing to explore them through their questions and observations. A conversation with Matthias raises the question as to what happens to those concerns, even preoccupations, later on.

I also located Klaus, now sixteen and living at a gymnasium in the northwestern part of West Berlin, where he had been for two years. It is a lovely location: a heavily wooded area along the Havel River where one could easily forget about the larger city of Berlin. Since we had last spoken, Klaus's life had taken some difficult and surprising turns. In 1985, after years of private suffering, Klaus's mother died. Although he had been living with his grandmother for several years and insists that he was never particularly close to his mother, he will concede, too, that her death was painful for him. It was not made easier by the continuing difficulties he encountered with his grandmother, so he made the decision to become a boarder at his gymnasium. Although he, too, has changed in significant ways, he has also remained the same. A talk with Klaus raises the knotty question of character, of its persistence through change and adversity.

You could write a whole book about my life. So much has happened to me. I remember telling you that I wanted to write a really harsh novel about family life; I think that was because I wanted to tell people about my own life. Well, I'd still like to write that book some day. I don't know when it will happen, though.

I really don't remember a lot of what I told you back then. I do know that I was very open when you last saw me. I spoke from the heart. Now, I'm sure I'd hesitate before answering a lot of those same questions. I've learned to keep some things to myself, to consider carefully before telling something important to someone. But I can tell you what happened to me after you left Berlin. I guess you can say I went through a fascist period in my life. At that age, I believe everyone looks for something to hold onto, something to believe in, to identify with. Some people are religious; some people believe in their social life, and go to dances and parties all the time. For me it was German history and politics. And then it was, like I said, military life. I got involved with other "fascist" kids, and for two years I almost always wore German army uniforms. You can buy them in the store and wear them wherever you want. Well, that's about all I ever wore. We'd hold maneuvers in the parks and in Grunewald. I did draw the line at hating, or hurting other people different from me. I was lucky I never needed to do that. But I look back on that period now and realize how much I needed that "something to hold on to."

I'm not sure how I began to come out of that. I came here to school, and people that I liked began to poke fun at me. But they weren't cruel with me, so slowly I began to relax and find other things to devote myself to. Part of the change, too, was that I was getting older. Things and people became important that weren't important before. I'd like to find a girlfriend, for one thing. And I've had to start thinking about what I want to do with my life. I know I don't want to stay here in Berlin; living here in the woods, I realize I'd be much happier in a village somewhere. I even consider moving to another country, Sweden for example, where I can do environmental research, which is what I'm now interested in.

Having held onto his vital curiosity and interest in the natural sciences, Klaus has managed to fashion an educational niche (and, he hopes, a later professional niche) for himself in the study of environmental protection. His life is a testimony to the struggle for meaning and for understanding and for purpose. In those terms, he has not changed very much at all. When he was twelve, he tried to make sense of the world, drawing on history and politics, in an effort to anchor himself. As he grew older, he continued to manifest this need for meaning but began to search for other objects of devotion. His is a story of resilience and endurance in the face of loss and suffering. It is also a story of the persistence of idealism and the various forms that idealism may take in a given life. Moving from the rigid, military idealism of his preadolescent days, Klaus now applies that moral energy to protecting his (our) world in other ways, through the application of his intellect and curiosity to environmental research. Speaking with Klaus, as with Matthias, raised the important question of what happens over time to an individual's political and moral curiosity and focus of attention.

Over in East Berlin there had been a number of changes as well. The entry through Checkpoint Charlie had been renovated and streamlined, presumably in anticipation of the twenty-fifth anniversary of the Wall and the 750th anniversary of Berlin. For the American tourist, at least, it is now somewhat easier to pass through security. Not once on this last trip was I asked to disclose the amount or kind of currency I was carrying with me into East Berlin. Five years ago that question was obligatory. Otherwise, the procedure of entering this city remains relatively the same.

Once through, I was surrounded by the sounds and sights of renovation and new construction, especially in the center of the city. Further out, in the direction of Prenzlauer Berg, for instance, the buildings remain as they have for almost a century, worn and scarred.

It was in this direction that I was headed when I passed by Oderbergerstrasse, a street that runs off of Kastanienstrasse and directly into the Wall. On this side, of course, the Wall (actually a secondary wall: there are mines, guards, dogs, etc. between this wall and the Wall as seen from West Berlin) retains its striking white facade—no opportunities here for graffiti (and if there were, what would it say?). Walking down the street, I was struck by the sight of several small children playing against the backdrop of this wall. As I approached them, heads and shoulders leaned out of the windows in apartments overhead. Not particularly friendly, but decidedly curious. As I got nearer to the children, one of them looked me squarely in the eye, waved, and came running up to me. We sat down on a curb, and as he began to interrogate me, I was once again a witness to the lessons a child has already begun to learn:

"Who are you?"

"My name?"

"Yes, and where are you from?"

"My name is Tom; I am from America."

"America?! What are you doing here?"

"I am visiting."

"Yes, but *how* did you get over here?"

"I walked here."

"A look of genuine consternation. "But we can't get over there; how did you get here?"

"There is an entrance at Checkpoint Charlie."

"There is an entrance?! Does that mean there is an entrance for us to go over there?"

"What do you think?"

"I don't think so. We cannot go over there."

"Why not?"

"Because the police won't let us. And because over there they want to take over our industry and ruin our factories."

"Would you like to visit?"

"Yes. I think so. I know I wouldn't like what they want to do with our factories . . . But I think everything is nicer over there. I hate our police here, because they won't let us over."

From this brief excerpt of a conversation with an eight-year-old boy we can see that his questions and obvious bafflement at some of my answers show the direct responses of the child, before he is entirely accustomed to this unusual situation. When he is a bit older, he will know more than to be surprised by those same answers. But unlike many of the children I'd known years ago, Michael lives directly up against the Wall. This means that his family is required to carry special identification cards, and that they are to have no contacts—friends or relatives—in the West. In addition, if anyone chooses to visit these people at home (otherwise designated as a "Grenzgebiet," or border area), including relatives or neighbors who live only a block or two away, they must apply to the authorities for a special visitor's pass. Although these families receive no special privileges for living under such conditions, they are at a decided disadvantage due to their lack of access to western currency or "connections." This living arrangement does offer a child like Michael certain consolation: he told me that he has a "job" with the border police. "If I ever seen anyone on the street here who does not belong here, then I run around the corner and wave to the police. Usually they come right away and get the person I tell them about." It is a "job" that leaves Michael feeling somewhat useful and important, but it is not without its conflicts as well. Although he works for the police (or thinks he does, or wishes to), he also has already identified them as responsible for keeping him on this side of the Wall. I suspect that the conflict will continue to exert its hold on him over the coming years. Again, I was reminded that "political socialization" takes many routes, and that children have already begun that journey at an early age.

I had this thought in mind as I continued on toward Torsten's house. His father has been relocated since we last spoke, and he now is minister to a congregation in the southern part of East Berlin. He continues to travel occasionally to western nations, and continues to offer what resistance he can to a government he is in strong disagreement with. Somehow he manages to walk that fine line between acceptable and unacceptable levels of criticism. Like many ministers of the Lutheran church in East Germany, he is now distressed by the declining church membership. Five years ago he had been optimistic, as increasing numbers of young people entered the church (if not always for explicitly religious reasons); now there appears to be a trend of leaving the church, although the reasons and the duration of this trend are not at all clear.

Torsten continues to be involved with the church, and he insists that he has his own reasons unrelated to the fact of his father's profession. "I grew up in that environment, where I was able to tell people what I am thinking, and where they could trust me, and each other, to do the same thing. It is still very important to me to be able to feel that kind of freedom, because otherwise where would I find it? The church still gives me something that I need . . . though it is also true that my involvement with the church may hurt me later when I try to get a job."

Torsten is now fifteen years old and in the ninth class at school. Like others his age, he has begun to think seriously of his future, of what he would like to do professionally. And he is already aware of the irony of his predicament. The church that has all along nurtured his idealism may also make it difficult for him to exercise that same idealism in a professional life. But he is thinking more and more of becoming a lawyer, though he is also aware of the difficulties he would face in a country that does not always respect human rights, or its own stated laws.

I know it might seem strange to you that I would want to work with the law after all I have learned from the church, from my father. But I think I must try to do something for people who have no one to help them. That is what my father does, as a minister. And my cousin is a lawyer too. I would like to be able to do the kind of work he does. He told me about someone he knows who has had a lot of problems with the government, and it is people like her that I would like to try to help. My cousin says she applied to leave the country a couple of years ago (you are allowed to make such an application, even though they punish you if you do), and as soon as that happened she lost her job, and her family—her father, her mother, her brother, everyone close to her—lost their jobs too. And they didn't let her leave, yet. She doesn't know if they will, or when. And if you don't work here, you go to jail. So my cousin says she has to sell ice cream or something. I have heard that kind of thing before; people always come to my father with stories of what the government does to them. And I think I should try to do something for them. You see, I can never forget where I am, and what I am allowed to do and not allowed to do. No one can forget here; you can try to get used to it, or *try* to forget . . . but if you have eyes and ears, you remember every day who is boss here, who can tell you what you can and can't do. Sometimes I do get depressed, and I know that even if I do become a lawyer, there will still be the government telling me where I can work, or that I still cannot visit the West. I see it in school all the time; how the teachers (not all of them, thank God) help the students who say the "correct" things, who have the right attitude. And it hasn't always helped me to have a father like mine. But I work hard in school, and so far it has been all right. My father says he gets depressed, too. Sometimes he wonders why he just keeps fighting like he does. But he also says that he would be even more depressed if he didn't do what he does. Maybe I'm a little like my father.

Certainly not all children retain the idealism expressed by Torsten as they get older. (Then again, not all children start out as idealistic, either.) Many become overwhelmed by the increasingly obvious limitations placed on their aspirations and their expectations. In listening to Torsten, I was struck by a crucial difference between him and his peers in West Berlin. In the West there is often the possibility (not always realized, of course) of leaving behind political or moral struggles with a government or a complicated, often painful set of national circumstances. Klaus can consider leaving for Sweden in order to carry on with his environmental research. Matthias can dream of living in Paris. Certainly they are still affected by the political world. They have internalized much of what they have witnessed and been taught: they are German children. Yet unlike Torsten and his peers in East Berlin, they need not be conscious on a daily basis of the influence of the political world. In East Berlin, politics is never abstract but has weight and form as it bears down on the day-to-day life of the individual. As Torsten says, "I can never forget where I am." Individuals see quite clearly how their decisions—personal and professional—are influenced by political reality, by a regime with a clear-cut ideological agenda, and the muscle to back it up.

Clearly it would be immensely valuable to do an extended follow-up study with these children as they go through adolescence. What happens over time to the political and moral struggles begun in earnest when these children were ten, eleven, or twelve? How will the idealism of children like Klaus or Torsten manifest itself in a few years? And where will the biting, satirical eye of Matthias take him as he grows older? These are questions that can only be answered "in the field," over an extended period of time. The task these children face is indeed complicated, and it is certainly not made easier by the confusing and demanding political and ideological circumstances in which they find themselves.

Notes

I Introduction

1. Jean-Jacques Rousseau, *The Government of Poland* (New York: Bobbs-Merrill, 1972), 20.

2. David Thomson, *Democracy in France,* 3d ed. (London: Oxford University Press, 1958), 143.

3. Several psychoanalytic theorists, among them Sigmund Freud, Erik Erikson, and Anna Freud, speak of latency as a significant developmental epoch, with its own tasks. Erikson refers to it as "socially a most decisive stage," in *Childhood and Society,* 2d ed. (New York: W. W. Norton, 1950), 260.

4. Anna Freud, *Normality and Pathology in Childhood* (New York: International Universities Press, 1965), 66.

5. Although Coles has made this observation consistently throughout his research career, he makes it most clearly and directly in his recently published books, *The Moral Life of Children* (Boston: Atlantic Monthly Press, 1986) and *The Political Life of Children* (Boston: Atlantic Monthly Press, 1986).

6. In addition to the varying amounts of attention paid to the salience of particular "agents" of political socialization, researchers vary considerably in the foci of their various searches. Some seek to examine the child's "sense of political efficacy": G. Almond and S. Verba, *The Civic Culture* (Boston: Little, Brown, 1965), and E. White, "Intelligence, Individual Differences, and Learning: An Approach to Political Socialization," *British Journal of Sociology* (March, 1969). Others speak of the child's "attitudes toward political authority": Fred Greenstein, *Children and Politics* (New Haven: Yale University Press, 1965); R. Hess and J. Torney, *The Development of Political Attitudes in Children* (Chicago: Aldine, 1967), and D. Jaros et al., "Transmitting Basic Political Values: The Role of the Educational System," *School Review* 77 (1969): 94–107. Still others refer to "party identification": M. Jennings and R. Niemi, "Patterns of Political Learning," *Harvard Educational Review* 38 (Summer 1968), and A. Kubota and R. Ward, "Family Influence and Political Socialization in Japan," *Comparative Political*

Studies 3 (1970): 140–75. Some concern themselves not with specific manifestations of political life but with the child's sense of nationality: W. Lambert and O. Klineberg, *Children's Views of Foreign Peoples* (New York: Meredith, 1967). D. Easton and J. Dennis, in "The Child's Image of Government," *American Academy of Political and Social Science, Annals* 361 (September 1965), postulate three aspects of political life, perhaps in an effort to synthesize the theoretical basis for further inquiry: the political community, the regime, and the authorities.

7. Greenstein, *Children and Politics;* Hess and Torney, *Political Attitudes in Children;* R. Sigel, "School Children's Reactions to the Death of a President," in *The Learning of Political Behavior,* ed. N. Adler and C. Harrington (New York: Scott, Foresman, 1970).

8. T. Okamura, "The Child's Changing Image of the Prime Minister," *Developing Economies* 6 (1968): 566–86; Jaros et al., "Transmitting Basic Political Values"; F. Rebelsky, "The Development of Political Attitudes in Young Children," *Journal of Psychology,* (1969): 73.

9. Jaros et al. "Transmitting Basic Political Values."

10. S. Bowers, "The Mobilization of Youth in Marxist East Germany," *Journal of Social and Political Studies* 5, no. 4 (1980): 163–82.

11. Although this is certainly a well-documented phenomenon, Saul Bellow treats it most effectively in *The Dean's December* (New York: Harper & Row, 1982).

12. Almond and Verba, *Civic Culture;* E. Litt, "Civic Education, Community Norms, and Political Indoctrination," in Adler and Harrington, eds., *The Learning of Political Behavior;* Hess and Torney, *Political Attitudes in Children;* K. Langton and M. Jennings, "Political Socialization and the High School Civics Curriculum in the United States," in Adler and Harrington, eds., *The Learning of Political Behavior;* Easton and Dennis, "The Child's Image of Government."

13. Eugene Weber, *Peasants Into Frenchmen* (Stanford: Stanford University Press, 1976), 303.

14. Urie Bronfenbrenner, *Two Worlds of Childhood: U.S. and U.S.S.R.* (New York: Simon & Schuster, 1970).

15. Laurence Wylie, *Village in the Vaucluse* (Cambridge: Harvard University Press, 1974), 208.

16. Until now little research has been conducted that is especially helpful in exploring the particular significance of the western media for the development of political values of East German youth. Rather, research (conducted in western nations, primarily England and the United States) had focused on the effect of "political programming" on voting behavior: J. Blumler and D. McQuail, *Television in Politics: Its Uses and Influence* (Chicago: University of Chicago Press, 1969); J. T. Klapper, *The Effects of Mass Communication* (New York: Free Press, 1960); H. Mendelsohn, "Some Reasons Why Information Campaigns Can Succeed," *Public Opinion Quarterly* 37 (1973–74). Also there have been examinations of the relationship between "political programming" and the development in the younger child of political attitudes: G. Byrne, "Mass Media and Political Socialization of Children and Pre-Adults," *Journalism Quarterly* 46 (1969); S. Chaffee, L. Ward, and L. Tipton, "Mass Communication and Political Socialization," in *Socialization to Politics,* ed. J. Dennis (New York: John Wiley & Sons, 1973); M. Johnson, "Television and Politicization: A Test of Competing

Models," *Journalism Quarterly* 50 (1973): 445; H. Tolley, *Children and War: Political Socialization to International Conflict* (New York: Teachers College Press, 1973). What all of these studies seem to suggest is that the medium is influential insofar as it affects the viewer's level of information regarding the political world, while exerting little appreciable influence on attitudes.

17. Piaget's work has been influential in the field of political socialization. See Piaget and Weil, "The Development in Children of the Idea of the Homeland and of Relations with Other Countries," *International Social Science Bulletin* 3 (1951). Having postulated a stagelike development of the sense of homeland corresponding to the child's cognitive and affective development, Piaget observed a shift from egocentricity to reciprocity, on both a cognitive and an emotional level. Young children appeared to confuse the relationship between town and country, finding it difficult to consider themselves citizens of both places simultaneously. Generally, by the age of ten, the relation between national part and whole became clear to these children. Piaget also noted three distinct stages of affective response to the nation: from the young child's preference for his country based on his own particular interests ("I like Switzerland because it has such pretty houses"), to a family-oriented preference ("I like Switzerland because I was born there, and my family is there"), to an identification with collective ideals of the national community ("I like Switzerland because it is a free country"). Lawrence Kohlberg, in "Moral Stages and Moralization," in *Moral Development and Behavior*, ed. T. Lickona (New York: Holt, Rinehart & Winston, 1976), also speaks of the child's active involvement in his increasingly elaborate construction of his or her (moral) world.

18. Anna Freud, *Normality and Pathology in Childhood*.

19. Piaget and Weil, "Idea of the Homeland"; J. Adelson, "The Political Imagination of the Young Adolescent," *Daedalus* 100 (Fall 1971): 1013–50; Kohlberg, "Moral Stages and Moralization."

20. Over the past several years I have visited each of these nations in order to speak with their children and to try to better understand what it means—politically, morally, psychologically—to grow up in complicated, potentially stressful and dangerous national circumstances.

21. Here I am reminded specifically of the work of Adelson, who worked with American youth, and Piaget, who worked with Swiss children.

22. In *Group Psychology and the Analysis of the Ego* (New York: Liveright, 1949), Freud traces the role of the ego ideal in group membership. He suggests that devotion to the object of the group replaces the functions of the ego ideal: "A primary group of this kind is a number of individuals who have substituted one and the same object for their ego ideal and have consequently identified themselves with one another in their ego" (p. 80).

23. John Mack, Introduction to *Cyprus—War and Adaptation*, by V. Volkan (Charlottesville: University Press of Virginia, 1979), xii.

24. Ibid., xiv.

2 Berlin

1. Gordon Craig, *The Germans* (New York; G. P. Putnam's, 1982), 266.

2. Jane Kramer, "A Reporter in Europe: West Berlin," *New Yorker*, December 7, 1981, 61.

3. "13 August 1961": *Seminarmaterial des Gesamtdeutschen Instituts;* Adenauerallee 10, 5300 Bonn I, FRG; August 4, 1981, 20.
4. Ibid., 34.
5. "The Berlin Wall: Fewer People Escape Each Year," *Norwalk Hour,* Norwalk, Conn.; October 28, 1983, 2.
6. *Heimatkunde: Lehrbuch Für Klasse 4* (Berlin: Volk und Wissen Volkseigener, 1982), 58.
7. Kramer, "A Reporter in Europe," 100.
8. Ibid., 57.
9. "357 Unfriedliche Demonstrationen im vergangenen Jahr," *Suddeutsche Zeitung,* June 18, 1982.
10. Kramer, "A Reporter in Europe," 58.
11. Ibid., 65.
12. "East Germany Puts King Back on His Pedestal," *New York Times,* December 14, 1980.
13. "Prussia Rediscovered in West German Display," *New York Times,* August 24, 1981.
14. "Ein prazises Feindbild Für DDR-Burger," *Der Tage Spiegel,* May 14, 1982.
15. "Church Backs Pacifism in E. Germany," *New York Times,* March 18, 1982.

3 Method

1. Here I have tried to follow the example of three superb clinicians and "fieldworkers": Anna Freud *(Normality and Pathology in Childhood),* Erik Erikson *(Childhood and Society),* and Robert Coles *(The Moral Life of Children* and *The Political Life of Children).*
2. Erik Erikson, *Childhood and Society* (New York: W. W. Norton, 1950).
3. Erik Erikson, *Insight and Responsibility* (New York: W. W. Norton, 1964), 53.
4. D. W. Winnicott writes sensitively and convincingly about this in his *Therapeutic Consultations in Child Psychiatry;* and Robert Coles relies heavily on children's drawings as a tool of his persistent moral, political and psychological investigations.

4 The Children of West Berlin

1. *Institut Für Demoskopie Allensbach,* 7753 Allensbach am Bodensee, Federal Republic of Germany; August 1981.
2. Ibid., March 1982.
3. Ibid., July 1981.
4. Ibid., 1979.
5. *New York Times,* February 22, 1982, A3.
6. *Institut Für Demoskopie Allensbach,* 1979.

5 The Children of East Berlin

1. "East Germany Loosens Up Through Contacts with West," *New York Times,* January 15, 1984.
2. Stephen Bowers, "The Mobilization of Youth in Marxist East Germany," *Journal of Social and Political Studies* 5, no. 4 (1980): 167. Dr. Guonter Hemling of the

GDR Academy of Pedagogical Sciences said just that in an article in the monthly journal *Junge Generation* (April 1976): "The education of youth into communist modes of thought and conduct is taking place within the process of constant and increasing confrontations with the ideology of imperialism."

3. Bowers, "Mobilization of Youth," 165.

4. Klaus Franke and Gerhard Krause, *Kommunisten und Jugend in der DDR* (Beverly Hills, Calif.: Sage Publications, 1975), 67–69.

5. *Frankfurter Rundschau,* December 13, 1978, 3.

6. *New York Times Magazine,* September 18, 1983, 43.

6 Conclusion

1. Walter Abish, *How German Is It?* (New York: New Directions, 1980), 171.

2. Gordon Craig, *The Germans* (New York: G. P. Putnam's, (1982), 332.

Bibliography

Abish, Walter. *How German Is It?* New York: New Directions, 1980.

Adelson, J. "The Political Imagination of the Young Adolescent," *Daedalus* 100 (Fall 1971): 1013–50.

Adelson, J., and R. O'Neil. "Growth of Political Ideas in Adolescence: The Sense of Community." *Journal of Personality and Social Psychology* 4 (1966): 295–306.

Adler, N., and C. Harrington. *The Learning of Political Behavior.* New York: Scott, Foresman, 1970.

Agee, Joel. *Twelve Years.* New York: Farrar, Straus & Giroux, 1981.

Akademie der Pädagogischen Wissenschaften der DDR. *Die Erziehung des jungeren Schulkindes.* Berlin: Volkseigener, 1976.

Almond, Gabriel. *The Civic Culture: Political Attitudes and Democracy in Five Nations, an Analytic Study,* with Sidney Verba. Boston: Little, Brown, 1965.

Ash, T. *Und Willst du Nicht Mein Bruder Sein: Die DDR heute.* Hamburg: Spiegel, 1981.

Aycoberry, P. *The Nazi Question.* New York: Pantheon, 1981.

Bellow, Saul. *The Dean's December.* New York: Harper & Row, 1982.

Bettelheim, B. *The Children of the Dream.* New York: Avon Books, 1969.

Blumler, J., and D. McQuail. *Television in Politics: Its Uses and Influence.* Chicago: University of Chicago Press, 1969.

Böll, H., Freimut Duve, and Klaus Staeck. *Verantwortlich Für Polen?* Hamburg: Rowohlt Taschenbuch, 1982.

Bossmann, D. *Was ich über Adolf Hitler gehört habe. . . .* Frankfurt am Main: Fischer Taschenbuch, 1977.

Bowers, Stephen. "The Mobilization of Youth in Marxist East Germany." *Journal of Social and Political Studies* 5, no. 4 (1980): 163–82.

Bronfenbrenner, U. *Two Worlds of Childhood: U.S. and U.S.S.R.* New York: Simon & Schuster, 1970.

Byrne, Gary. "Mass Media and Political Socialization of Children and Pre-adults." *Journalism Quarterly* 46 (1969): 140.

Carr, W. *A History of Germany, 1815–1945.* 2d ed. New York: St. Martin's Press, 1979.

Chaffee, S., L. Ward, and L. Tipton. "Mass Communication and Political Socialization." In *Socialization to Politics,* edited by J. Dennis. New York: John Wiley & Sons, 1973.

Coles, R. "Children and Political Authority." In *The Mind's Fate.* Boston: Atlantic–Little, Brown, 1975.

―――. *Children of Crisis: A Study of Courage and Fear.* Boston: Atlantic–Little, Brown, 1964.

―――. *Migrants, Sharecroppers, Mountaineers.* Boston: Atlantic–Little, Brown, 1972.

―――. *The Moral Life of Children.* Boston: Atlantic Monthly Press, 1986.

―――. *The Political Life of Children.* Boston: Atlantic Monthly Press, 1986.

―――. *Privileged Ones: The Well Off and Rich in America.* Boston: Atlantic–Little, Brown, 1977.

―――. "Ulster's Children." *Atlantic Monthly,* December, 1980.

Comstock, G., et al. *Television and Human Behavior.* New York: Columbia University Press, 1971.

Connell, R. W. *The Child's Construction of Politics.* Melbourne: Melbourne University Press, 1971.

Craig, Gordon. *The Germans.* New York: G. P. Putnam's, 1982.

Davies, J. C. "The Family's Role in Political Socialization." *American Academy of Political and Social Science, Annals* 361 (September 1965): 10–19.

Dennis, J. *Socialization to Politics: A Reader.* New York: John Wiley & Sons, 1973.

Der Tage Spiegel, West Berlin, May 14, 1982.

Deutscher Bundestag. *Fragen an die deutsche Geschichte.* Bonn: Deutscher Bundestag, 1981.

Deutschland, Deutschland: 47 Schriftsteller aus der BRD und der DDR schreiben über ihr Land. Hamburg: Rowohlt Taschenbuch, 1981.

Doob, L. *Patriotism and Nationalism.* New Haven: Yale University Press, 1964.

Easton, D., and J. Dennis. "The Child's Image of Government." *American Academy of Political and Social Science, Annals* 361, (September 1965): 40–57.

―――. *Children in the Political System: Origins of Political Legitimacy.* New York: McGraw-Hill, 1969.

―――. "The Child's Political World." In *The Learning of Political Behavior,* edited by N. Adler and C. Harrington. New York: Scott, Foresman, 1970.

Erikson, E. *Childhood and Society.* New York: W. W. Norton, 1950.

―――. *Insight and Responsibility: Lectures in the Ethical Implications of Psychoanalytic Insight.* New York: W. W. Norton, 1964.

―――. *Young Man Luther.* New York: W. W. Norton, 1958.

―――. *Gandhi's Truth.* New York: W. W. Norton, 1969.

F., Christianne. *Wir Kinder vom Bahnhof Zoo.* Hamburg: Stern Magazin, 1979.

Fitzgerald, F. *America Revised.* Boston: Atlantic Monthly Press, 1979.

Flessau, Kurt-Ingo. *Schule der Diktatur.* Frankfurt am Main: Fischer Taschenbuch, 1979.

Franke, K., and G. Krause. *Kommunisten und Jugend in der DDR.* Beverly Hills, Calif.: Sage Publications, 1975.

Frankfurter Rundschau. 13 December 1978.

Freud, A. *Normality and Pathology in Childhood.* New York: International Universities Press, 1965.

———. *Infants Without Families and Reports on the Hampstead Nurseries, 1939–1945,* with D. Burlingham. London: Hogarth Press, 1974.

Freud, S. *Group Psychology and the Analysis of the Ego.* New York: Liveright, 1949.

———. *Civilization and Its Discontents.* New York: W. W. Norton, 1961.

———. "Mourning and Melancholia." In *The Complete Psychological Works of Sigmund Freud.* Vol. 14. London: Hogarth Press, 1915.

Frost, Robert. *The Poetry of Robert Frost.* New York: Holt, Rinehart and Winston, 1975.

Geiger, Kent. "Changing Political Attitudes in Totalitarian Society." *World Politics* 8 (1955–56): 187–205.

Geschichte der Freien Deutschen Jugend. Berlin: Neues Leben, 1982.

Greenstein, F. *Children and Politics.* New Haven: Yale University Press, 1965.

Greenstein, F., and S. Tarrow. "The Study of French Political Socialization." *World Politics* 22 (1969–70): 95.

Halperin, S. W. *Germany Tried Democracy.* New York: W. W. Norton, 1946.

Handke, P. *Kindergeschichte.* Frankfurt am Main: Suhrkamp Verlag, 1981.

Havemann, R. *Berliner Schriften.* Munich: Deutscher Taschenbuch, 1977.

Heimatkunde: Lehrbuch Für Klasse 4. Berlin: Volk and Wissen Volkseigener, 1982.

Hess, R. "The Socialization of Attitudes Toward Political Authority: Some Cross-National Comparisons." *International Social Science Journal* 15 (1963): 542–59.

Hess, R., and J. Torney. *The Development of Political Attitudes in Children.* Chicago: Aldine, 1967.

———. "The Family and School as Agents of Socialization." In *The Learning of Political Behavior,* edited by N. Adler and C. Harrington. New York: Scott, Foresman, 1970.

Hobbes, T. *Leviathan.* Oxford: Blackwell Press, 1955.

Hyman, H. *Political Socialization.* Glencoe, Ill.: Free Press, 1959.

Ikehata, S. "Jose Rizal: The Development of the National View of History and National Consciousness in the Philippines." *Developing Economies* 6 (1968): 176–92.

Inhelder, B., and J. Piaget. *The Growth of Logical Thinking from Childhood to Adolescence.* New York: Basic Books, 1958.

Institut Für Demoskopie Allensbach, 7753 Allensbach am Bodensee, Federal Republic of Germany: 1981, no. 5 ("Lieb Vaterland . . . ?"); no. 15 ("Der Pfahl Im Fleisch Der DDR"); no. 23 ("Brauchen Wir Eine Fahne?"); 1982, no. 2 ("Helmut Schmidt and Die SPD"); no. 5 ("Die Deutschen"); no. 6 ("Die Frage Nach Dem Nationalstolz der Deutschen"); no. 10 ("Wahlalter 18 oder 21?")

Isherwood, C. *The Berlin Stories.* New York: New Directions, 1945.

Jaros, D., and B. Canon. "Transmitting Basic Political Values: The Role of the Educational System." *School Review* 77 (1969): 94–107.

Jennings, M., and R. Niemi. "Patterns of Political Learning." *Harvard Educational Review* 38, no. 3 (Summer 1968).

———. "The Transmission of Political Values from Parent to Child." *American Political Science Review* 62 (1968): 169–84.

Johnson, M. "Television and Politicization: A Test of Competing Models." *Journalism Quarterly* 50 (1973): 445.

Junge Generation 4 (1976). For further information on *Junge Generation,* write to Haus des Lehrers, Alexanderplatz, Berlin, GDR.

Klapper, J. T. *The Effects of Mass Communication.* New York: Free Press, 1960.

Koehn, I. *Mischling, Second Degree: My Childhood in Nazi Germany.* New York: Greenwillow Books, 1977.

Kohlberg, L. "Moral Stages and Moralization." In *Moral Development and Behavior,* edited by Thomas Lickona. New York: Holt, Rinehart and Winston, 1976.

Kramer, Jane. "A Reporter in Europe: West Berlin." *New Yorker,* December 7, 1981.

Kubota, A., and R. Ward. "Family Influence and Political Socialization in Japan." *Comparative Political Studies* 3 (1970): 140–75.

Kunze, R. *The Wonderful Years.* New York: Braziller, 1977.

Lambert, W., and O. Klineberg. *Children's Views of Foreign Peoples.* New York: Meredith, 1967.

Langton, K. and M. Jennings. "Political Socialization and the High School Civics Curriculum in the United States." In *The Learning of Political Behavior,* edited by N. Adler and C. Harrington. New York: Scott, Foresman, 1970.

Lawson, E. "Development of Patriotism in Children—A Second Look." *Journal of Psychology* 55 (1963): 279–86.

Litt, E. "Civic Education, Community Norms, and Political Indoctrination." In *The Learning of Political Behavior,* edited by N. Adler and C. Harrington. New York: Scott, Foresman, 1970.

Locke, J. *Two Treatises of Government.* New York: Hafner, 1947.

Mack, J. *A Prince of Our Disorder: The Life of T. E. Lawrence.* Boston: Little, Brown, 1976.

––––––. Introduction to *Cyprus—War and Adaptation,* by V. Volkan. Charlottesville: University Press of Virginia, 1979.

Mendelsohn, H. "Some Reasons Why Information Campaigns Can Succeed." *Public Opinion Quarterly* 37 (1973–74): 50–61.

Money-Kyrle, R. E. *Psychoanalysis and Politics.* New York: W. W. Norton, 1951.

Moore, B. *Injustice: The Social Bases of Obedience and Revolt.* White Plains, N.Y.: M. E. Sharpe, 1978.

New York Times, December 14, 1980; February 22, 1982; March 18, 1982; January 15, 1984.

New York Times Magazine, September 18, 1983.

Norwalk Hour, Norwalk, Conn., October 28, 1983.

Okamura, T. "The Child's Changing Image of the Prime Minister." *Developing Economies* 6 (1968): 566–86.

Panorama DDR, *Fragen and Antworten: Leben in der DDR.* Berlin: Panorama DDR, 1981.

Pelikan, Jaroslav. "The Enduring Relevance of Martin Luther 500 Years After His Birth." *New York Times Magazine,* September 18, 1983, 43.

Piaget, J. "The Development in Children of the Idea of the Homeland and of Relations with Other Countries." *International Social Science Bulletin* 3 (1951): 561–78.

––––––. *The Moral Judgment of the Child.* New York: Free Press, 1965.

Pieper, K. *Um 6 Uhr Steh ich auf: Kinder aus der DDR erzählen.* Berlin: Der Kinderbuch, 1979.

Plato. *The Republic.* Baltimore: Penguin Books, 1976.

Pye, L. *Politics, Personality, and Nation Building.* New Haven: Yale University Press, 1962.

Rebelsky, F., et al. "The Development of Political Attitudes in Young Children." *Journal of Psychology* 73 (November 1969): 141–46.

Reich, W. *The Mass Psychology of Fascism.* New York: Farrar, Straus & Giroux, 1970.

Rousseau, J. *Emile.* London: Dent, 1969.

―――. *The Government of Poland.* Indianapolis: Bobbs-Merrill, 1972.

Schädlich, K. M., and F. Werner. *Die Hälfte der Stadt: Ein Berliner Lesebuch.* Munich: Athenaum, 1982.

Schneider, Peter. *The Wall Jumper.* New York: Pantheon Books, 1983.

Shirer, W. *Berlin Diary.* New York: Penguin Books, 1941.

Siegel, R. "Assumptions About the Learning of Political Values." *American Academy of Political and Social Science, Annals* 361 (September 1965): 1–9.

―――. "School Children's Reactions to the Death of a President." In *The Learning of Political Behavior,* edited by N. Adler and C. Harrington. New York: Scott, Foresman, 1970.

Spradley, James P. *Participant Observation.* New York: Holt, Rinehart and Winston, 1980.

Steinitz, V., et al. "Ideological Development in Working Class Youth." *Harvard Educational Review* 43, no. 3 (August 1973): 333–61.

Suddeutsche Zeitung, 18 June 1982.

"13 August 1961." *Seminarmaterial des Gesamtdeutschen Instituts;* Adenauerallee 10, 5300 Bonn I, FRG, August 4, 1981.

Thomson, D. *Democracy in France.* 3d ed. London: Oxford University Press, 1958.

Tolley, H. *Children and War: Political Socialization to International Conflict.* New York: Teachers College Press, 1973.

Volkan. V. *Cyprus—War and Adaptation.* Charlottesville: University Press of Virginia, 1979.

Vond der Grün, Max. *Wie war das eigentlich? Kindheit und Jugend im Dritten Reich.* Darmstadt: Luchterhand, 1979.

Wald, K. *Children of Che.* Palo Alto: Ramparts Press, 1978.

Weber, E. *Peasants Into Frenchmen.* Stanford: Stanford University Press, 1976.

White, E. "Intelligence, Individual Differences, and Learning: An Approach to Political Socialization." *British Journal of Sociology* (March 1969): 50–68.

Winnicott, D. W. *Therapeutic Consultations in Child Psychiatry.* New York: Basic Books, 1971.

Wolf, Christa. *A Model Childhood.* New York: Farrar, Straus & Giroux, 1980.

Wylie, L. *Village in the Vaucluse.* Cambridge: Harvard University Press, 1974.

Zentralinstitut Für Geschichte der Akademie der Wissenschaften der DDR. *Grundriss der deutschen Geschichte.* Berlin: VEB Deutscher Verlag der Wissenschaften, 1979.

Index

About the Author

Thomas Davey is a psychologist in Boston who has worked primarily with children and adolescents. He has also taught literature, psychology, and religion courses at Harvard for several years. He has travelled extensively—to South Africa, Poland, Israel, Northern Ireland, and, of course, East and West Berlin—in order to better understand the political and moral development of children living in extreme political and social circumstances.